# A WORLD OF WISDOM

## Fun and Unusual Phrases from Around the Globe

# A WORLD OF WISDOM

Fun and Unusual Phrases from Around the Globe

## DR. JAMES CHAPMAN

Andrews McMeel
PUBLISHING®

# WHAT IS THE WORLD TO YOU?

"The world is your oyster."
*(English)*

"The world is your canvas."
*(Spain, Colombia)*

"The world is at your feet."
*(Germany)*

"The world is at your service."
*(Russia)*

HOTEL DU MONDE

"The world is your hotel."
*(Pakistan)*

HEY!

"The world is a pot;
man, a spoon in it."
*(Armenia)*

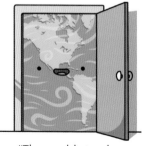

"The world stands
open before you."
*(Poland)*

TAKE CARE OF YOURSELF

"The world is the
world for the world."
*(Japan)*

# INTRODUCTION

When thinking about different cultures and places, we usually focus on the food, the people, and the landscape. Language is an important part of any culture, too. Expressions like proverbs and idioms passed down through generations can tell us so much about life in a specific place.

Proverbs are little nuggets of wisdom that impart a moral or message, and idioms are figurative turns of phrase that have a meaning beyond their literal one. For example, in English-speaking countries we might say, "it's raining cats and dogs," and it means that it's raining very hard, not that house pets are falling from the sky. But when there's a heavy rainstorm in Slovakia, they say it "rains tractors," and in Colombia, it "rains husbands!"

This book is a collection of these kinds of marvelous phrases from all over the globe, shining a light on the subtle differences found in our lives and the cultures we come from.

Take apples, for example; they're common in so many countries. Apple juice, apple pie; apples are everywhere! They're common in English expressions too—such as in phrases like "the apple of your eye" and "an apple a day keeps the doctor away." Living in such an apple-loving culture, it makes sense that they show up so frequently, right?

But what if apples aren't so common, though? Venezuela is one of the biggest pineapple producers in the world. So in that country, an annoying person isn't called "a bad apple" or "a pain in the neck," but instead they're *eres una piña bajo el brazo*, "a pineapple under the arm." It's a perfect fruit-based description for an uncomfortable annoyance.

The phrases in this book illustrate these kinds of ideas in wonderfully unexpected ways, as well as unique concepts you may not already know.

After all, the world is a diverse place, full of knowledge everywhere you turn. There's a world of wisdom out there!

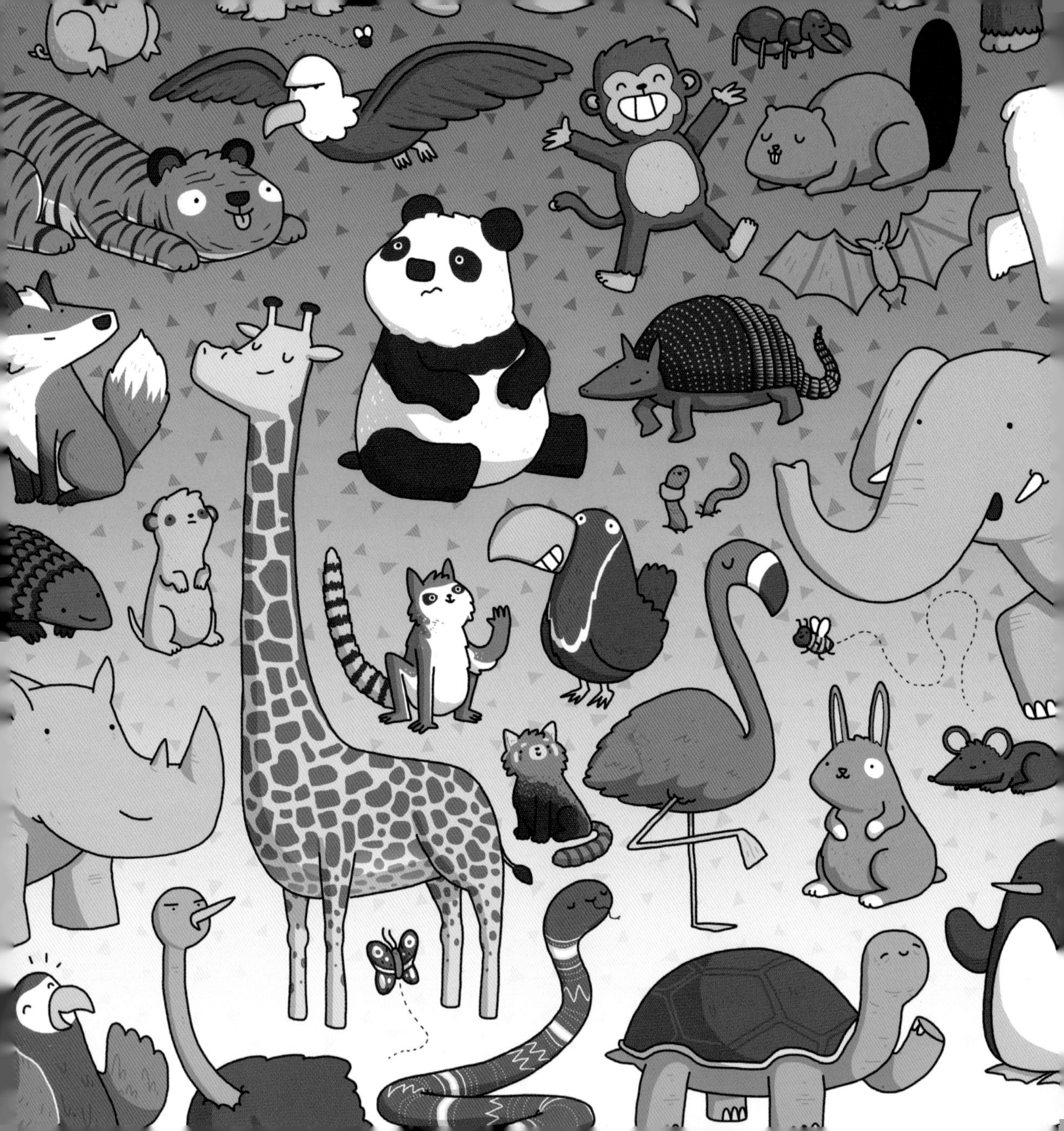

# THE ANIMAL KINGDOM

You don't always encounter the same animals as you move around the world, and the creatures people see on a daily basis are reflected in different countries' expressions.

English phrases often refer to farmyard animals and domestic pets, and there aren't many sayings about tigers as there aren't too many around. Across East Asia, however, tigers are a bit more common, and so East Asian sayings have more of them, too.

This is a look into the more exotic animals that have become proverbial stars around the world. From African elephants to the bears of Norway, these creatures are full of wisdom!

**"WHEN ELEPHANTS FIGHT, IT IS THE GRASS THAT GETS HURT."**

*"Wapiganapo tembo nyasi huumia."* **Kenya**

Thousands of elephants live in Kenya, and they feature in a Swahili phrase or two. This refers to the dangers of careless government. When the powerful fight, it's usually vulnerable people who suffer.

# "TWO TIGERS CANNOT SHARE A MOUNTAIN."

"一山不容二虎." *China*

Just like the old Wild West cliché, "this town ain't big enough for the both of us," this is all about the inevitable conflict between big personalities.

## "EVEN RABBITS DREAM OF THE MOON."

"กระต่าย หมาย จันทร์." *Thailand*

Aspirations are important, and even the smallest of us can be motivated by big dreams.

## "A WORM WANTS TO BE A DRAGON."

*"Cacing hendak menjadi naga."* **Indonesia**

Another tale of aspiration, from nearby Indonesia. This time it's the humble worm who wants to grow into a mighty dragon. It's an ambitious goal, but those are the best ones to strive for!

## "THE BEAR AND THE BEAR-HUNTER HAVE DIFFERENT OPINIONS."

*"Bjørnen og bjørnemannen har ikkje same meining."* **Norway**

Arguments between those with completely opposite opinions—like
bears and their hunters—can often be unsolvable.

## "WHEN SPIDERWEBS UNITE, THEY CAN TIE UP A LION."

*"ድር ቢያብር አንበሳ ያስር."* **Ethiopia**

Teamwork is key to taking down seemingly impossible challenges.

## "A TORTOISE TRAVELS WITH ITS INSTRUMENT IN CASE IT MEETS OTHER MUSICIANS."

*"Eze mbe si na ihe ya ji-achiri ihe egwu ya aga njem bu maka ya ezu ndiegwu."* **Nigeria**

Always be prepared for whatever might come over the horizon. Whether you're going to school or to summer camp, take what you need (in case you come across a tortoise to rock out with).

## "A SNAKE HAS NO BAGGAGE."

*"Snek nɔ gɛt bɔndul."* **Sierra Leone**

In contrast to the musical tortoise who's always prepared for any eventuality, this saying favors a lighter way of travelling. The less baggage you have the more freedom you can enjoy.

## "THERE'S MORE THAN ONE DONKEY CALLED MARTIN AT THE FAIR."

*"Il y a plus d'un âne à la foire qui s'appelle Martin."* **France**

Not a phrase that's used as much anymore, this one is all about jumping to conclusions. Martin is a common name for French donkeys, so it's best not to assume which Martin is which.

## "THE EAGLE DOES NOT WAGE WAR AGAINST FROGS."

*"Le aquile non fanno guerra ai ranocchi."* **Italy**

When it comes to conflict, pick your battles. If you consider yourself a proud eagle, getting upset with frogs is a waste of time.

"THERE'S PLENTY OF FISH IN THE SEA."

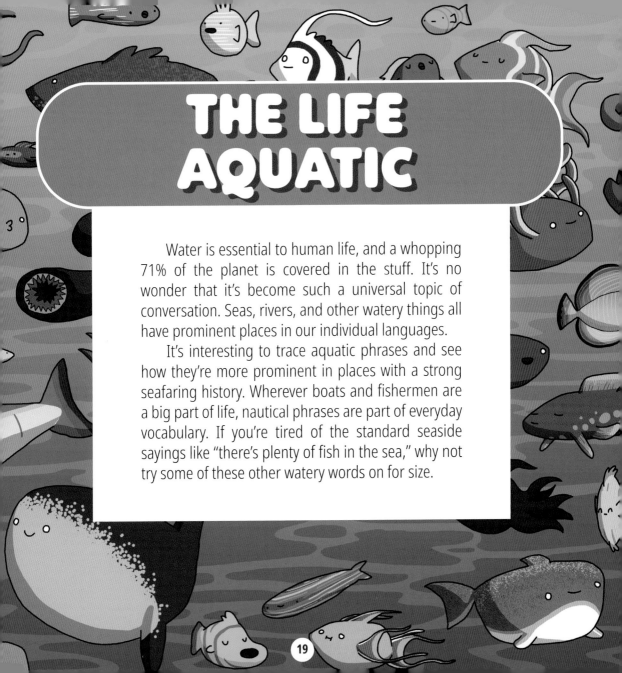

# THE LIFE AQUATIC

Water is essential to human life, and a whopping 71% of the planet is covered in the stuff. It's no wonder that it's become such a universal topic of conversation. Seas, rivers, and other watery things all have prominent places in our individual languages.

It's interesting to trace aquatic phrases and see how they're more prominent in places with a strong seafaring history. Wherever boats and fishermen are a big part of life, nautical phrases are part of everyday vocabulary. If you're tired of the standard seaside sayings like "there's plenty of fish in the sea," why not try some of these other watery words on for size.

"A FROG IN A WELL KNOWS NOTHING OF THE GREAT SEA."

"井の中の蛙大海を知らず." *Japan*

A warning that if you don't look at the big picture, you'll miss out.
Always seek to expand your horizons, and you'll be a better-informed frog/person.

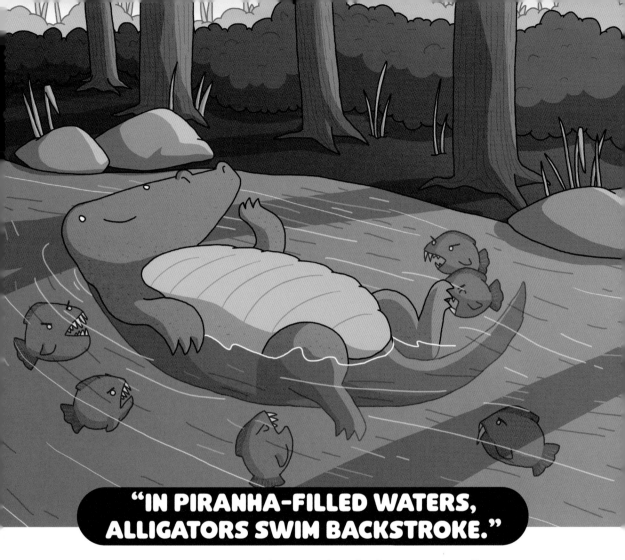

## "IN PIRANHA-FILLED WATERS, ALLIGATORS SWIM BACKSTROKE."

*"Em rio que tem piranha, jacaré nada de costas."* **Brazil**

Alligators have tough backs but soft bellies, so they ought to be careful swimming with ravenous piranhas below. It's important to know your weaknesses and, even more importantly, know how to protect yourself.

## "DON'T COMPLAIN ABOUT TOO LITTLE WIND—LEARN TO SAIL."

*"Klaga inte över för lite vind—lär dig segla."* **Sweden**

If you can make the most of a tough situation, you can do great things in the face of adversity. As Francis Bacon says, "A wise man will make more opportunities than he finds."

## "IN THE CALMEST WATERS, SWIM THE UGLIEST FISH."

*"I de lugnaste vattnen simmar de fulaste fiskarna."* **Sweden**

Another take on the idea that appearances can be deceiving. Those who appear calm and tranquil on the surface might be villainous deep down. Though the opposite might be true, and an ugly fish could be a sweetheart!

## "A DRAGON CAN RISE UP FROM A STREAM."

"개천에서 용 난다." *South Korea*

A saying that suggests success can come from unexpected places. Dragons are good luck in Korean culture, often depicted as rising up from the ocean, but sometimes even a humble stream can birth great things.

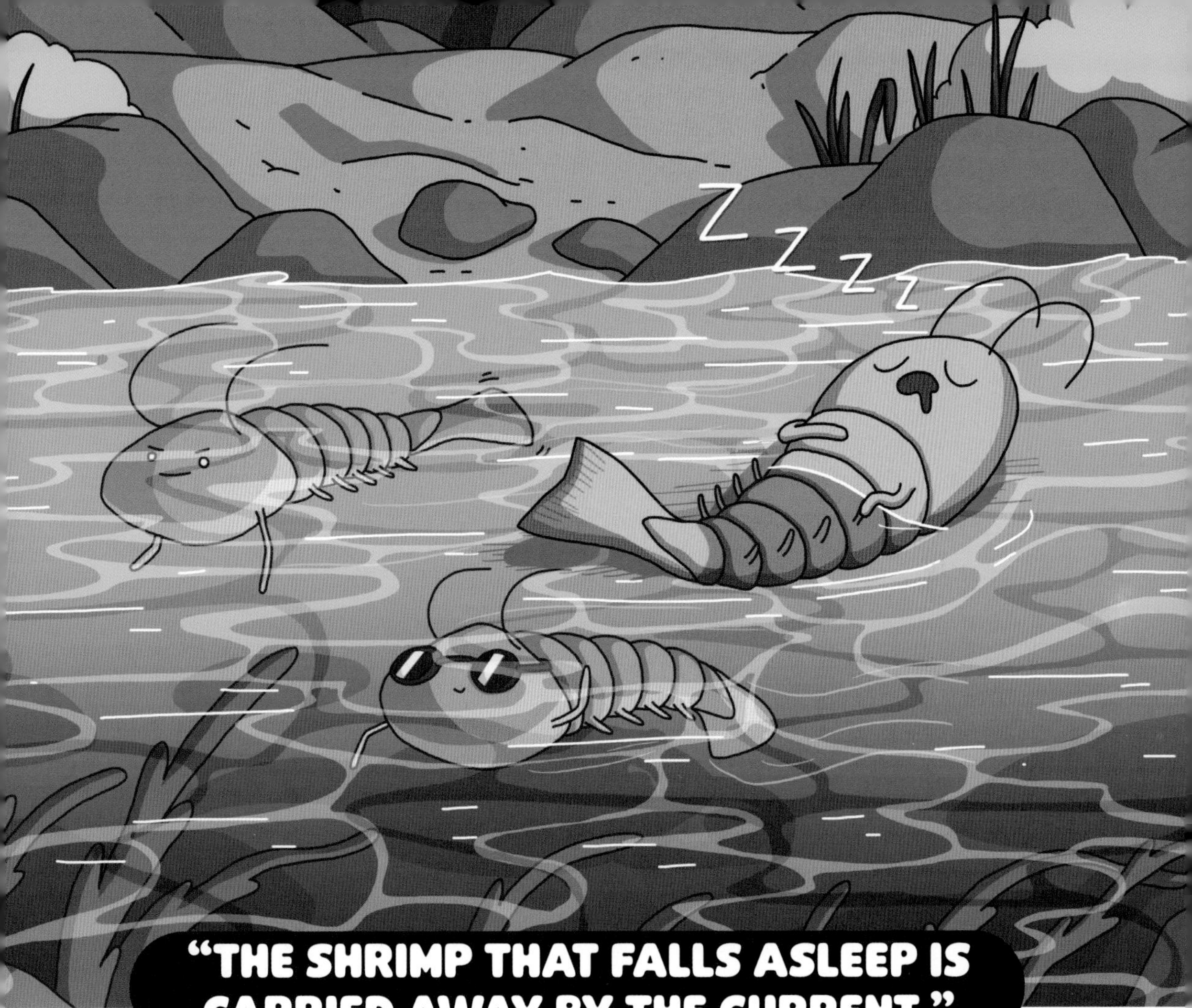
ZZZZ

## "THE SHRIMP THAT FALLS ASLEEP IS CARRIED AWAY BY THE CURRENT."

*"Camarón que se duerme se lo lleva la corriente."* ***Spain, Argentina***

If you're lazy, you won't get where you want to be, so stay alert and focused to accomplish your goals.

# "CURIOSITY KILLED THE CAT."

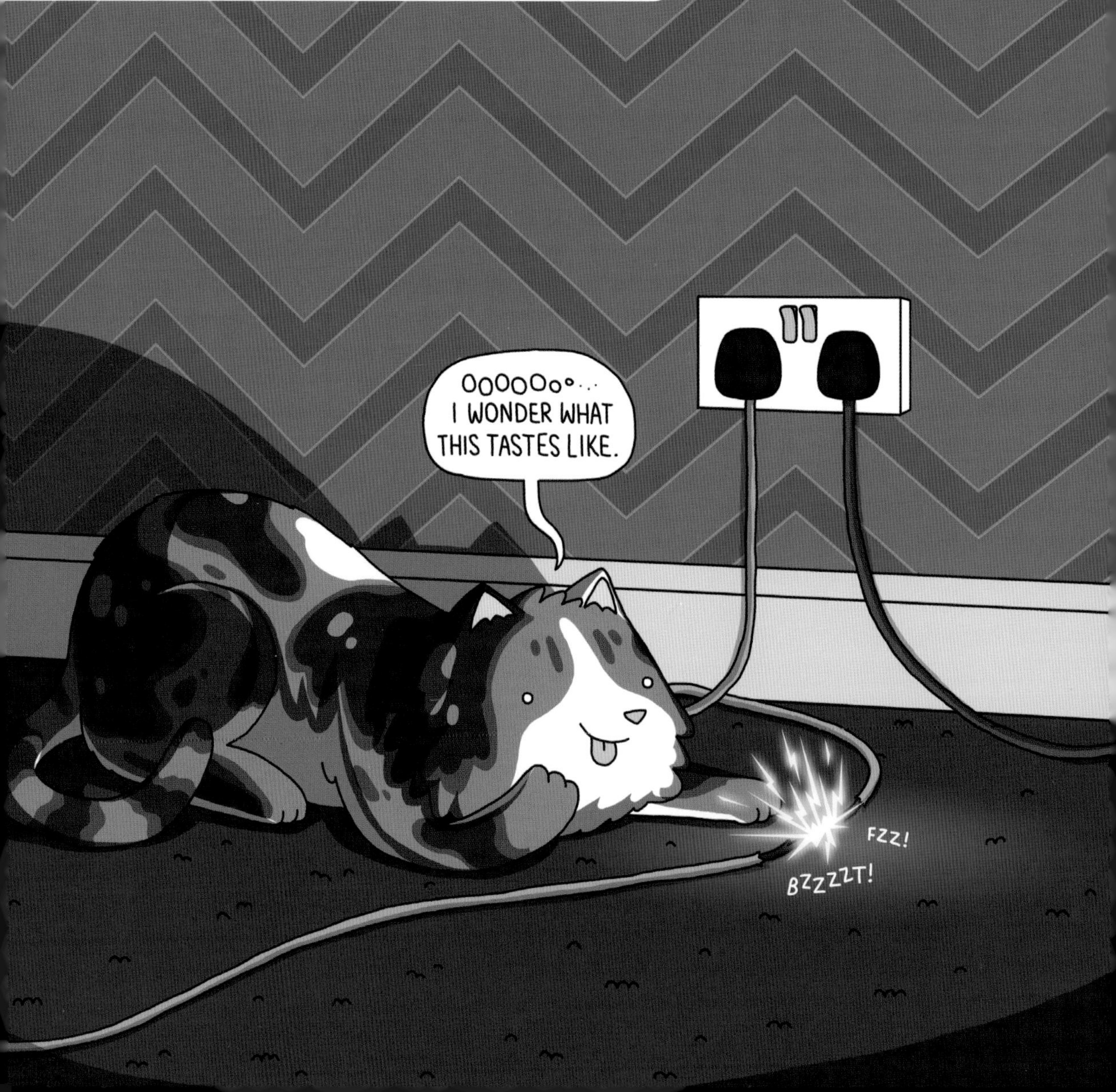
OOOOOOo...
I WONDER WHAT
THIS TASTES LIKE.
FZZ!
BZZZZT!

# CATS

Cats are wonderful. But aside from sleeping, eating, and getting hair everywhere, they don't really do a lot. So why do we love them so much? It's simple—they're cute, they're fluffy, they're companionable, and they're uniquely suited to internet videos. This might explain why there's one cat for every four people in the United States, for a total of 76.5 million cats! That's more than the population of the UK.

With such popularity, it's no wonder cats feature heavily in language. So here's to the fluffy friends and the international joy they bring!

## "THE CAT DREAMS OF THE FINEST CUTS OF MEAT."

"बिल्ली को छीचड़ो के ख्वाब." *India*

Dreams can inspire you to achieve things beyond your normal grasp. Cats are often fed leftovers, but they have aspirations that one day they could eat the highest quality food.

## "THOSE WITHOUT A DOG, HUNT WITH A CAT."

*"Quem não tem cão, caça com gato."* **Brazil**

When facing adversity, it's best to try to adapt to the situation. If you don't have a hunting dog, change your tactics. Either train your cat to hunt or, as some interpret this, learn to hunt in a catlike way.

## "DON'T ENTRUST A CAT WITH A FISH."

*"고양이에게 생선을 맡기다." **South Korea***

Like "don't swim with sharks," this expression is pure common sense.
Simply put, don't trust the untrustworthy.

## "ACCUSATION FOLLOWS THE CAT."

**Iraq** "التهيمة لا حكة البزونة"

If something goes wrong and you need someone to blame, you can't go wrong blaming the cat.
Innocent or not, if whoever you're accusing can't defend themselves, they're an easy target.

## "EVEN CATS WANT SHOES."

*"Hasta los gatos quieren zapatos."* **Spain**

Another proverb about the fancy dreams cats have every time they take a nap. Ambition is a powerful thing, even if some dreams—like adorable cat shoes—are more unlikely than others.

## "A CAT HAS NO BUSINESS IN A DOG FIGHT."

*"Puss nuh business inna dawg fight."* **Jamaica**

Some fights are none of your business, and you probably shouldn't stick your nose in. Much like a curious cat, you might be tempted to get involved, but you're better off steering clear.

# WHEN THE CAT'S AWAY, THE MICE WILL PLAY

For phrases in original languages, see the appendix on page 198.

With roots in Latin, this phrase began as "dum felis dormit, mus gaudet et exsi litantro"—"when the cat sleeps, the mouse rejoices and leaps from its hole". Mousey activities are the subject of sayings all around the world, and without the watchful cat, they're doing it all!

BOING!

"When the cat's away, the mice jump on the table." (Finland)

"When the cat's away, the mice dance." (France)

"When the cat's away, the mice have a party." *(Brazil)*

"When the cat's away, the mice throw javelins." *(Turkey)*

"When the cat's away, the mice have freedom." *(Russia)*

FREEDOM!

CHEESY LOVER

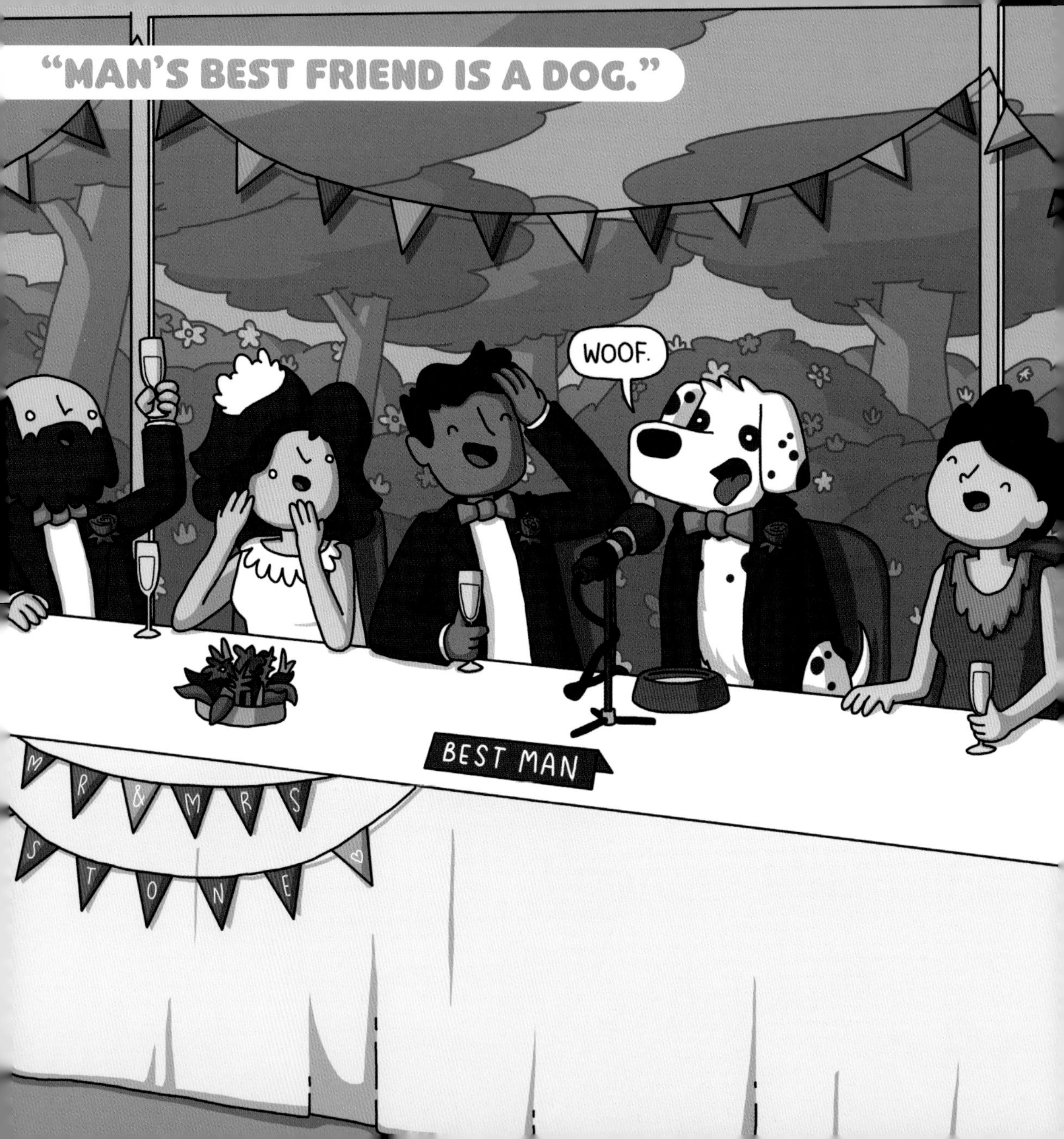
"MAN'S BEST FRIEND IS A DOG."
WOOF.
BEST MAN
MR & MRS
STONE

# DOGS

Dogs are the world's most popular pet, and with over 400 million of them across the globe, you can't go far without seeing one.

With this level of popularity, people just can't stop talking about them, and dozens of doggy sayings have worked their way into every day expressions around the world.

They've gained the reputation as "man's best friend" in English, but let's see how other places talk about our four-legged friends.

**"BETTER TO BE A DOG AT PEACE THAN A MAN IN CHAOS."**

"寧為太平犬, 不做亂世人." *China*

This is a phrase that encourages an uneventful but reliable lifestyle. While the ups and downs of a chaotic life might be exciting, a peaceful life can be very enjoyable free from dramatic changes.

## "IF YOU FOLLOW A DOG, IT'LL LEAD YOU TO A RUBBISH HEAP."

*"We yu fala dɔg, i kɛr yu go na dɔti bɔks." Sierra Leone*

Following those with motives different from your own can get you off track. Dogs have a keen sense of smell and are attracted to the strongest odor. If you let them lead, you might end up in a bit of a stink.

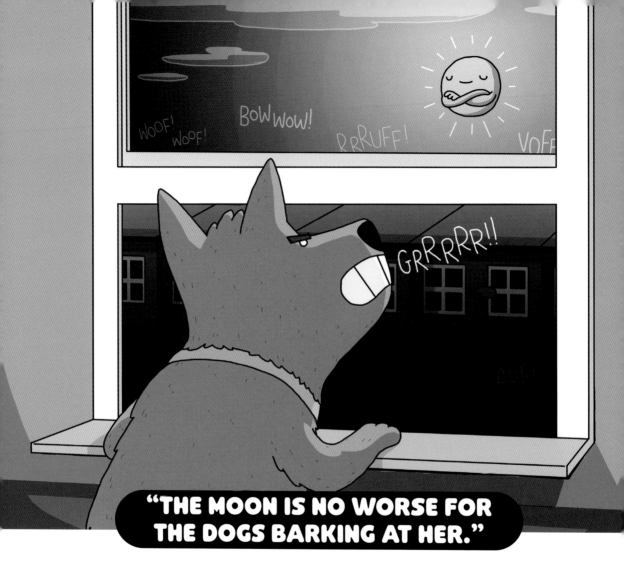

## "THE MOON IS NO WORSE FOR THE DOGS BARKING AT HER."

*"Cha mhisd' a' ghealach na coin a bhith comhartaich rithe."* **Ireland**

Don't worry about the criticisms of others; just keep doing your thing. The moon doesn't give a hoot about the opinions of dogs—she's having a great time spinning around in space.

# "TOO MUCH PUDDING WILL CHOKE A DOG."

*"Gormod o bwdin dagith gi."* **Wales**

Too much of a good thing can be bad for you. That goes double for dogs and desserts as chocolate can actually be quite dangerous for them. Make sure you eat all your pudding so the dogs can't get any.

## "THE DOG IS PROPELLED BY ITS TAIL."

*"Wanambwa asukumungwa nende okushira kukwe."* **Kenya**

Dogs can be so full of energy—absolute whirlwinds of fluff. But where does all that energy come from? It's an international mystery, but this old Kenyan phrase has an idea that sounds quite believable.

## "A DOG BITTEN BY A SNAKE IS AFRAID OF SAUSAGES."

*"Cão picado por cobra, tem medo de linguiça."* **Brazil**

After you've been hurt, you're often careful to not let it happen again. If you've had a run-in with a snake, it's only natural to double-check any snake-like sausages to be on the safe side.

# “LAUGHTER IS THE BEST MEDICINE.”

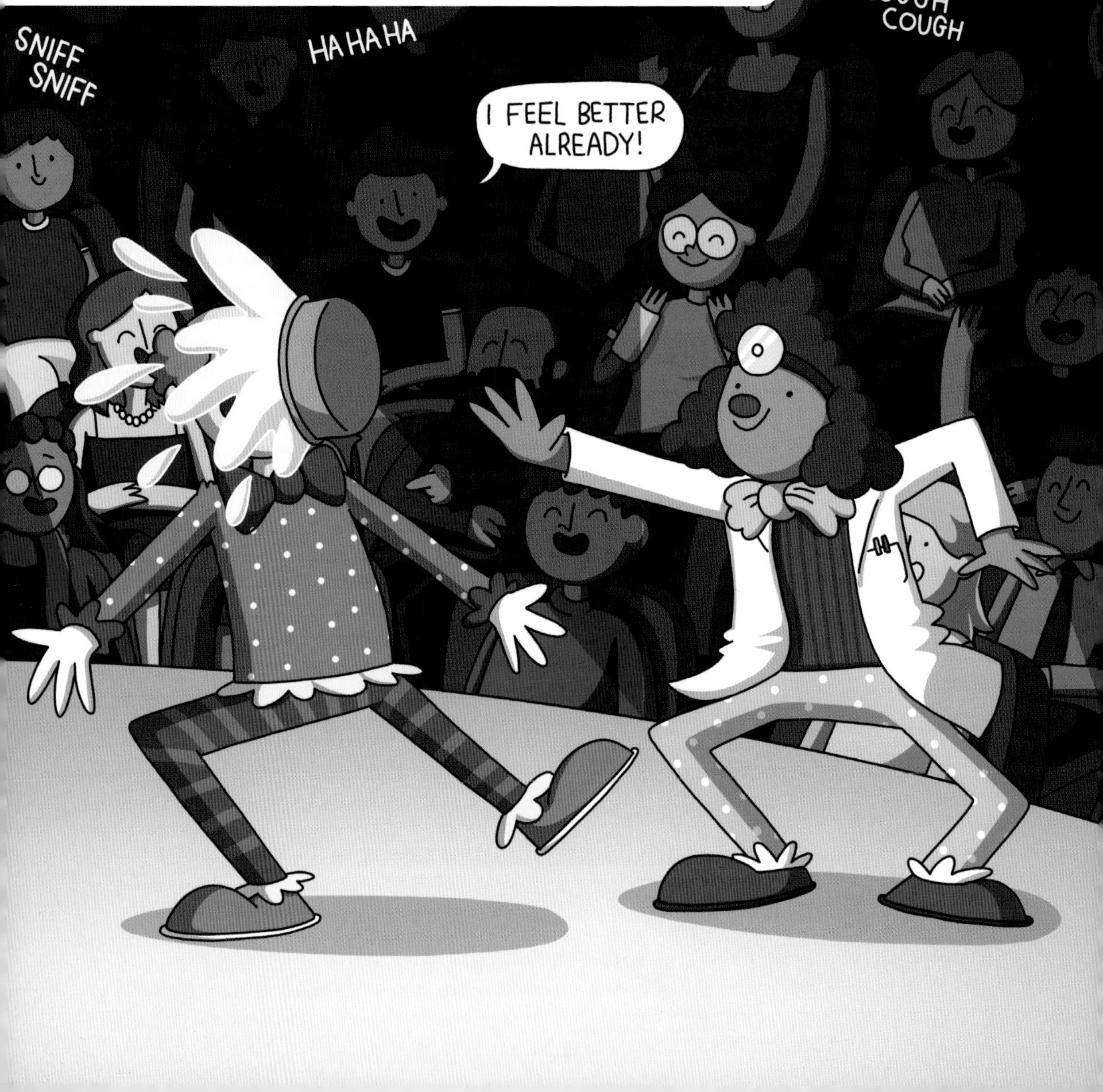
SNIFF SNIFF
HA HA HA
COUGH COUGH
I FEEL BETTER ALREADY!

# FUNNY PEOPLE

As cultures seemingly change from place to place, people often still act the same way in certain situations. Whether it's making excuses like a bad workman blaming his tools, or exaggerating a problem and making a mountain out of a molehill.

The phrases we use to describe these behaviors change around the world, but they are all different ways of talking about the same parts of human nature.

People can act so funnily wherever you go, and that's something to be celebrated with these expressions. After all, laughter is the best medicine.

# ONCE BITTEN, TWICE SHY

It's important to learn from your mistakes so you won't make the same ones again (even if you can end up being overly cautious, like a dog who's scared of sausages). As another saying goes, "fool me once, shame on you, fool me twice, shame on me."

OH NO! I'VE BEEN BITTEN!

NOW I'M... **SHY!**

"A donkey only goes on the ice once."
*(Slovenia)*

"One doesn't step on the same rake twice."
*(Estonia)*

THIS PROBABLY WON'T END WELL...

BONK!

"A spooked crow is scared of a bush."
*(Russia, Ukraine, Belarus)*

RUSTLE RUSTLE

"A burnt child shuns the fire."
*(Germany, Austria, Denmark, Norway, Iceland, Sweden, and Old English)*

"A scalded cat fears cold water."
*(France, Italy, Portugal, Spain)*

"Those bitten by a snake are afraid of worms."
*(Slovakia)*
*Even more snake phrases are found in China, Brazil, Hungary and Czech Republic.*

"Whoever burns their tongue on porridge will blow on yogurt."
*(Greece)*
*More burnt tongues too in India, Poland, Turkey, Egypt, Romania, Serbia, Croatia, and Ireland*

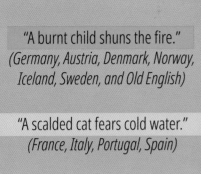

AH!

GUMMI WORMS NEW

YUM!

WHOOOOSH

BURNT CHILDREN

SPOOKED CROWS

WET CATS

SNAKES

HOT PORRIDGE AND MILK

(MORE SNAKES)

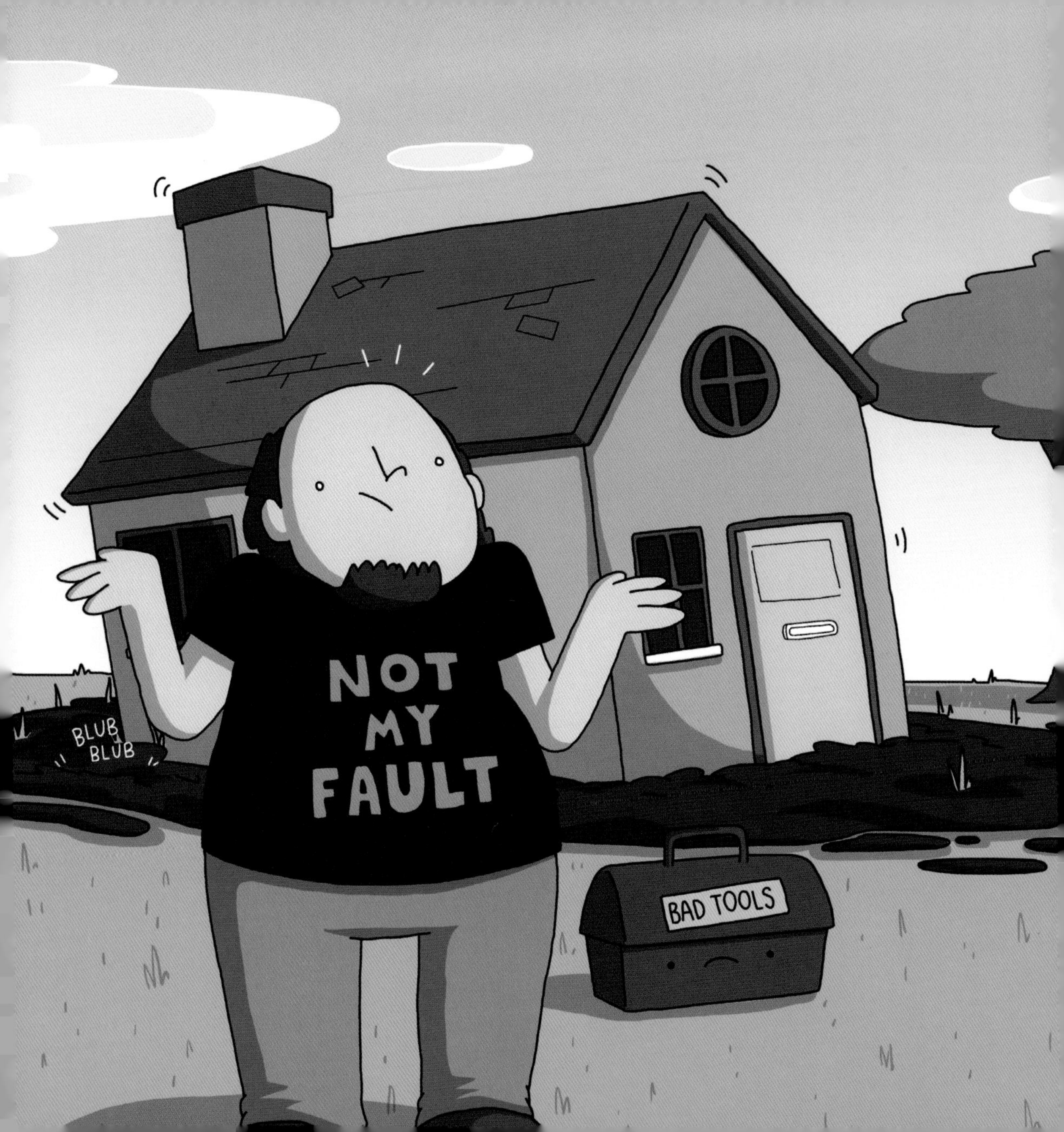
BLUB
BLUB
NOT
MY
FAULT
BAD TOOLS

# A BAD WORKMAN BLAMES HIS TOOLS

Let's see how the world looks at excuses. "A bad workman blames his tools" is a phrase in the English language that calls out those who try to shift blame away from themselves when they do something wrong. Excuses are international though, and wherever you are in the world, you can't avoid them. The sentiment about blame-shifters is the same all over but the way it's phrased changes from place to place.

## "A BAD BALLERINA BLAMES THE HEM OF HER SKIRT."

*"Zlej baletnicy przeszkadza rabek u spodnicy."* **Poland**

While bad workmen are the go-to example in English, different professions capture the imaginations of other cultures, and in Poland, it's shifty ballerinas.

# "THOSE WHO CAN'T DANCE SAY THE GROUND IS SLOPING."

*Iraq* "اللي ميعرف يرگص يگول الگاع عوجة"

It turns out dance moves are a common focus of excuses in many places. In Malaysia, bad dancers are said to say "the floor is a seesaw," to excuse their lackluster moves.

## "THE BAD WRITER BLAMES THE PEN."

*"El mal escribano le echa la culpa a la pluma."* **Spain**

In Spain, it's writers, not dancers who like to shift the blame. Variations are also used in Germany, and even South Korea, where it's translated as "a good calligrapher doesn't blame the writing brush."

## "WHEN THE RIDER'S NO GOOD, IT'S THE HORSE'S FAULT."

"Wenn der Reiter nichts taugt, hat das Pferd Schuld." **Germany**

Again, there's a similar expression in Spain that used to be quite common:
"When the wagon driver is bad, he blames the donkey."

## "A BAD ROWER BLAMES THE OAR."

*"Árinni kennir illur ræðari."* **Iceland**

Since Iceland is an island nation with a rich seafaring history, it's no wonder
bad rowers and their oars show up in this proverb, still used today.

## "A GOOD PLOUGHMAN CAN PLOUGH EVEN WITH A GOOSE."

*"Geras artojas ir su žąsinu paaria."* **Lithuania**

Some countries take a more positive angle. In Lithuania, a bad workman may blame his equipment, but a good one can get the job done with a mere goose in his toolbox.

# THE POT CALLING
# THE KETTLE BLACK

Some people point out faults in others that they're guilty of having too. Much like a burnt kitchen pot telling the kettle it needs a wash, it's not a polite thing to do. It's best to be aware of your own faults before criticizing. This phrase dates back as far as the 1600s in English, and it'll likely be around for years to come, even with these great alternatives around.

"The dog calling the cat hairy."
(Vietnam)

"The armadillo telling
the turtle it's too hard-shelled."
*(Venezuela)*

"The Roquefort telling
the Camembert it stinks."
*(France)*

YUCK!

HA HA HA HA HA HA HA HA HA

"A monkey
laughing at
another's
red butt."
*(Japan)*

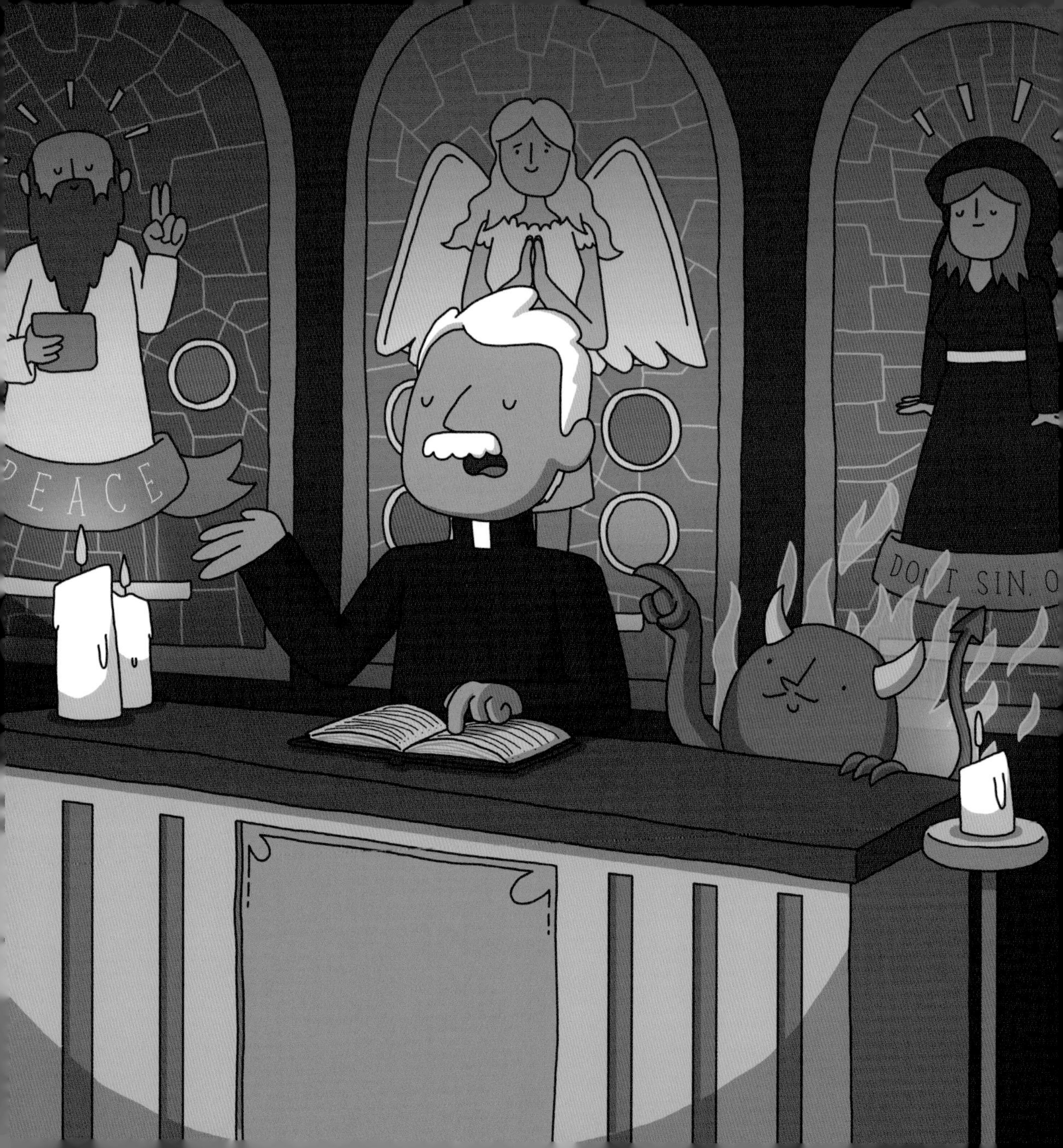
PEACE

# SPEAK OF THE DEVIL, AND HE SHALL APPEAR

Has the person you're talking about ever turned up in front of you while you were still talking about them? It's such a common occurrence that equivalent phrases to "speak of the devil" turn up in almost every language.

The English version of this phrase started in the Middle Ages to refer to a superstition that speaking about the devil would lead to bad luck, but its meaning has since evolved to how we use it today.

Around the world, however, the expression focuses on all manner of different characters. From cats and trolls to kings and tigers, things just won't stop appearing as soon as you mention them!

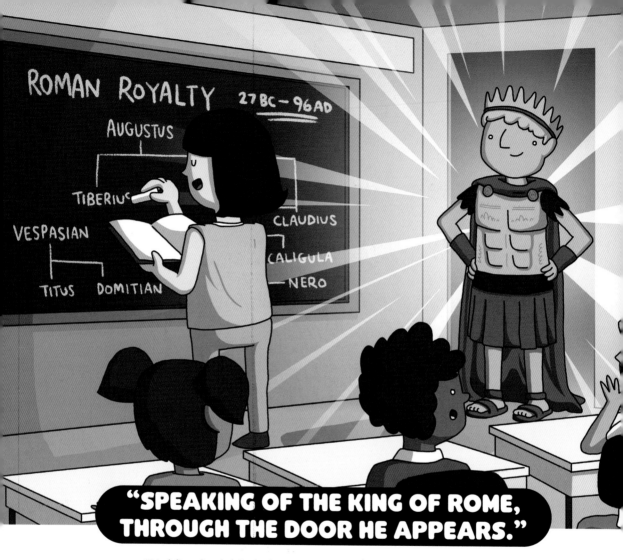

## "SPEAKING OF THE KING OF ROME, THROUGH THE DOOR HE APPEARS."

*"Hablando del Rey de Roma, por la puerta asoma."* **Spain**

In the 1300s, there was a run of very unpopular Popes, so instead of "speak of the devil," people spoke of bad Popes, known as "the ruin of Rome." This later became "the King of Rome" as the Pope's image improved.

## "MENTION THE CAT AND HE'LL COME JUMPING."

"جبنا سيرة القط، جاء ينط" *Egypt*

Cats are huge in Middle Eastern culture—it was in this region they were first domesticated 10,000 years ago—so this feline-centric Egyptian phrase is very appropriate.

## "WHEN YOU SPEAK OF THE TROLLS, THEY STAND IN THE ENTRANCE HALL."

*"När man talar om trollen, så står de i farstun."* **Sweden**

In Swedish culture, trolls are a big part of the folklore, and they're not necessarily the brightly colored cuties you might be thinking of. In this case, they're something you'd rather keep away from, much like the devil.

"GOSSIP ABOUT SOMEONE AND THEIR SHADOW WILL APPEAR."

"うわさをすれば影." *Japan*

This is similar to a phrase in China; if you gossip about
"people in the day or ghosts at night," they'll suddenly appear.

## "SPEAK OF THE WOLF AND IT'S IN THE SHEEP PEN."

*"Говорим за вълка, а той в кошарата."* **Bulgaria**

Wolves are a popular subject for this saying, always turning up to bother the sheep. Similar expressions are found across Eastern Europe, and as far away as Saudi Arabia.

## "EVEN THE TIGER WILL APPEAR WHEN SOMEONE SPEAKS OF IT."

*"호랑이도 제 말하면 온다." **South Korea***

Tigers are sacred figures in Korean culture, driving away evil spirits and bringing good luck. As recently as 100 years ago, they were found in the wild too, often enough that they showed up in this old saying.

# MAKING A MOUNTAIN OUT OF A MOLEHILL

A great phrase for when someone's overreacting, it has been around since 1548. Initially, from an English biblical translation, "make an elephant of a flye, and a mountaine of a molehill," it's hung around ever since. Here are some great exaggerations from other countries.

NEARLY... THERE...

"Drown in a spoon of water."
*(Greece)*

"See a mosquito, and draw a sword."
*(South Korea)*

"Make a dome out of a bump."
*(Egypt)*

"Make a mountain out of a grain of sand." (Spain)

"Make a fork out of a needle." (Poland)

"Make an elephant out of a fly." (Italy, Russia, Slovenia)

"Make an elephant out of a mosquito." (The Netherlands)

"Make a camel out of a mosquito." (Czech Republic) *or a louse in Armenia, and a gnat in Iceland*

"Make a storm in a glass of water." (Brazil)

"Make a cheese out of it." (France)

"Make a hen out of a feather." (Sweden) *In Norway, it's said you're making **five** hens.*

# BIG TALK

Some people love to talk about their big ideas but have no plan to put them into action. In the US, variations of this idea from "all sizzle, no steak" to "all hat, no cattle" are common. But it's an international idea, and wherever you go, there will always be people full of big talk.

BLAH
BLAH
BLAH

"All mouth and no trousers."
*(Great Britain)*

"All smoke and nothing roasted."
*(Italy)*

STILL RAW

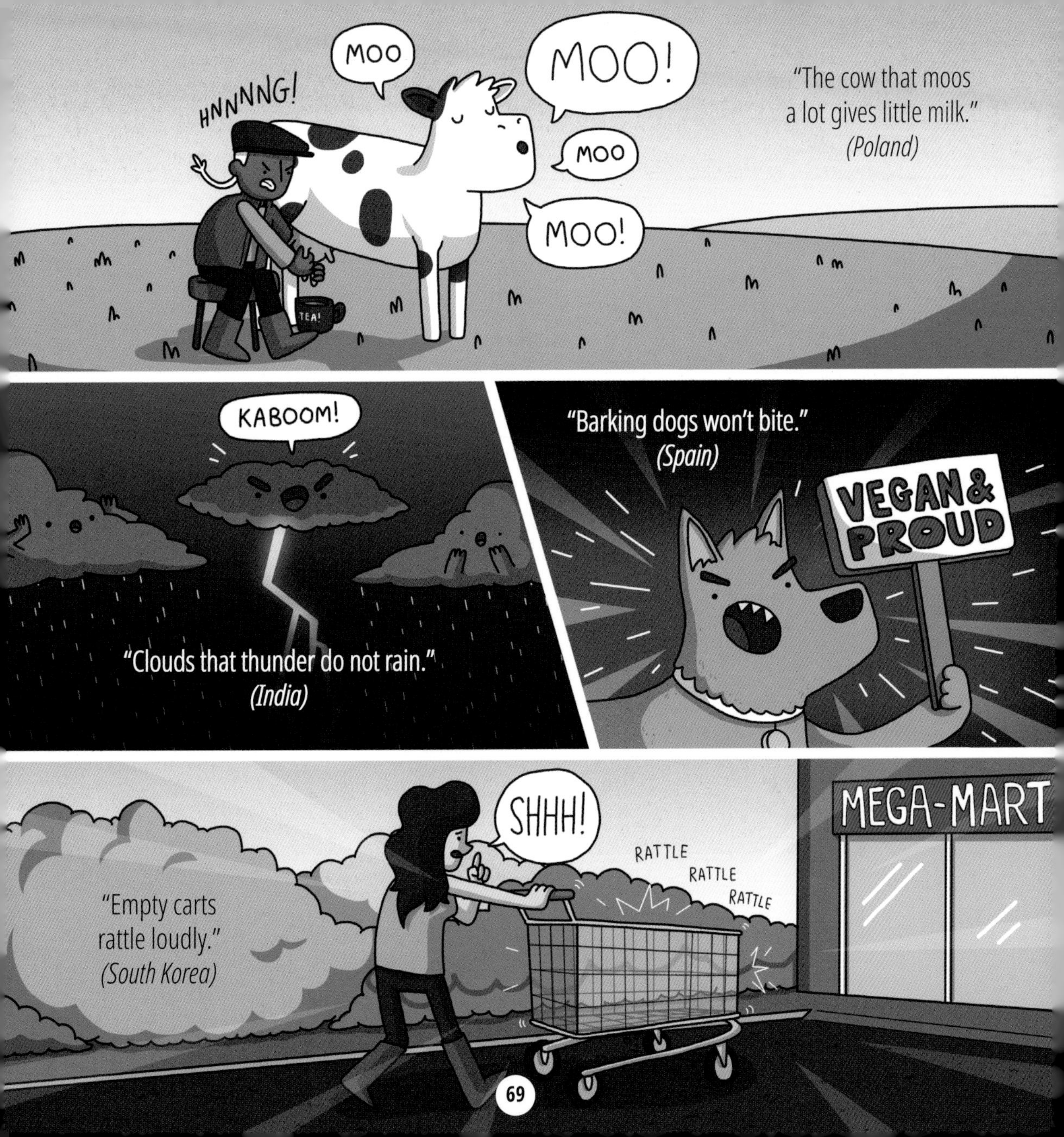
HNNNNG!
MOO
MOO!
MOO
MOO!
TEA!
"The cow that moos a lot gives little milk."
(Poland)
KABOOM!
"Clouds that thunder do not rain."
(India)
"Barking dogs won't bite."
(Spain)
VEGAN & PROUD
SHHH!
RATTLE
RATTLE
RATTLE
MEGA-MART
"Empty carts rattle loudly."
(South Korea)

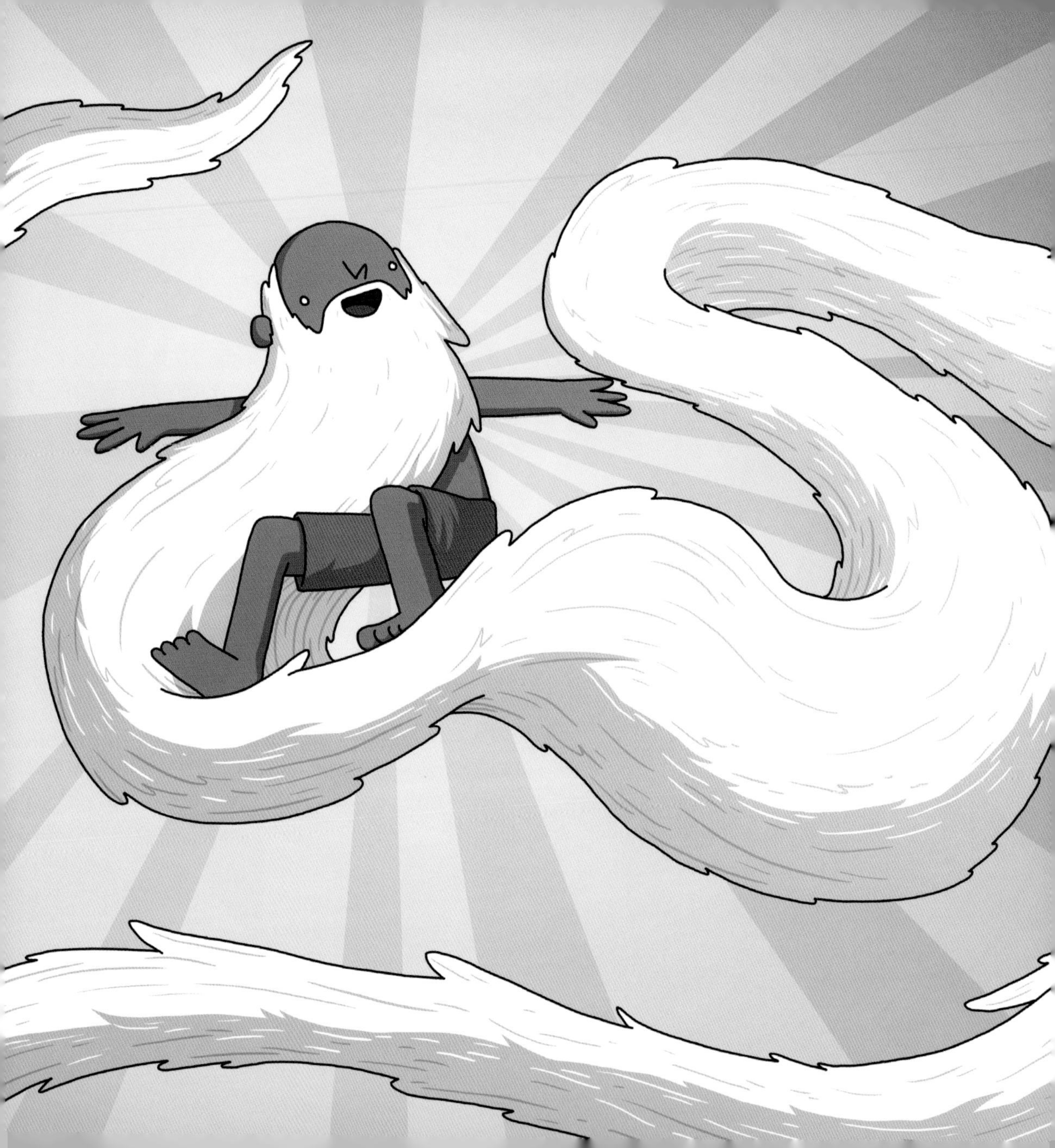

# FACIAL HAIR

Beards and mustaches may seem ever so stylish these days, but they're not universally popular.

In China and Japan, facial hair can be considered a bit messy, and it's not very fashionable to have any. But in places like India, some religions, like Sikhism, forbid shaving altogether, leaving followers with some beautifully bushy beards.

Here are some delightful beardy expressions to start working into your conversations.

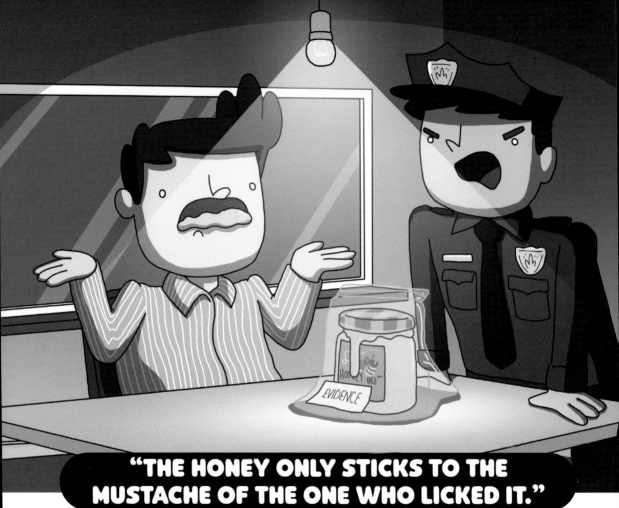

## "THE HONEY ONLY STICKS TO THE MUSTACHE OF THE ONE WHO LICKED IT."

"لدبس مايلطا الا بشارب لاحسه" *Saudi Arabia*

A much more delicious version of being caught "red-handed," if you commit a crime, the evidence will stick to you like honey to a 'stache.

## "WHOEVER HAS THE BEARD HAS THE COMBS."

*"Όποιος έχει τα γένεια, έχει και τα χτένια."* ***Greece***

If you have a glorious beard, surely some combs are nearby. The message being,
if you need something, ask whoever is best suited to help you.

## "A MAN WITHOUT A BEARD IS LIKE BREAD WITHOUT CRUST."

*"Vyras be barzdos, kaip duona be plutos."* **Lithuania**

Beards are a big deal in Lithuania. In fact, the world record for most weight lifted with a beard is held by Lithuanian Antanas Kontrimas, who lifted a 140lb woman with his!

## "WHEN YOU SEE YOUR NEIGHBOR'S BEARD BURNING, PUT YOURS IN WATER."

*"Cuando veas las barbas de tu vecino arder, mete la tuya en remojo."* **Venezuela**

Taking caution when others are in trouble is only natural. If someone's
beard is on fire, you'd better jump in the pond.

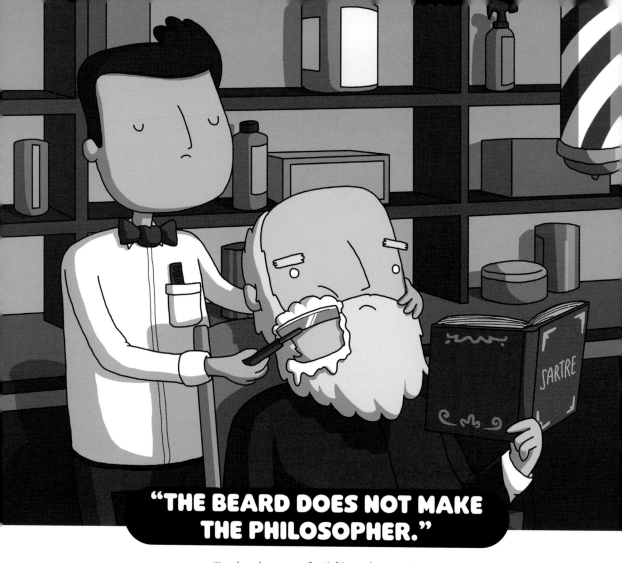

## "THE BEARD DOES NOT MAKE THE PHILOSOPHER."

*"La barba non fa il filosofo."* **Italy**

Appearances can be deceiving; those with smooth faces can be just as wise as those with stately beards.
This phrase, which originated in Latin, suggests looking beneath the surface to see what people are really like.

## "MUSTACHES ARE RESPECTED, BUT BEARDS ARE WORN EVEN BY GOATS."

*"Ус в честь, а бородá и у козлá есть."* **Russia**

The age-old dispute: beards vs. mustaches . While this saying goes one way, another Russian version is little more beard friendly: "beards are respected, but mustaches are worn even by cats.

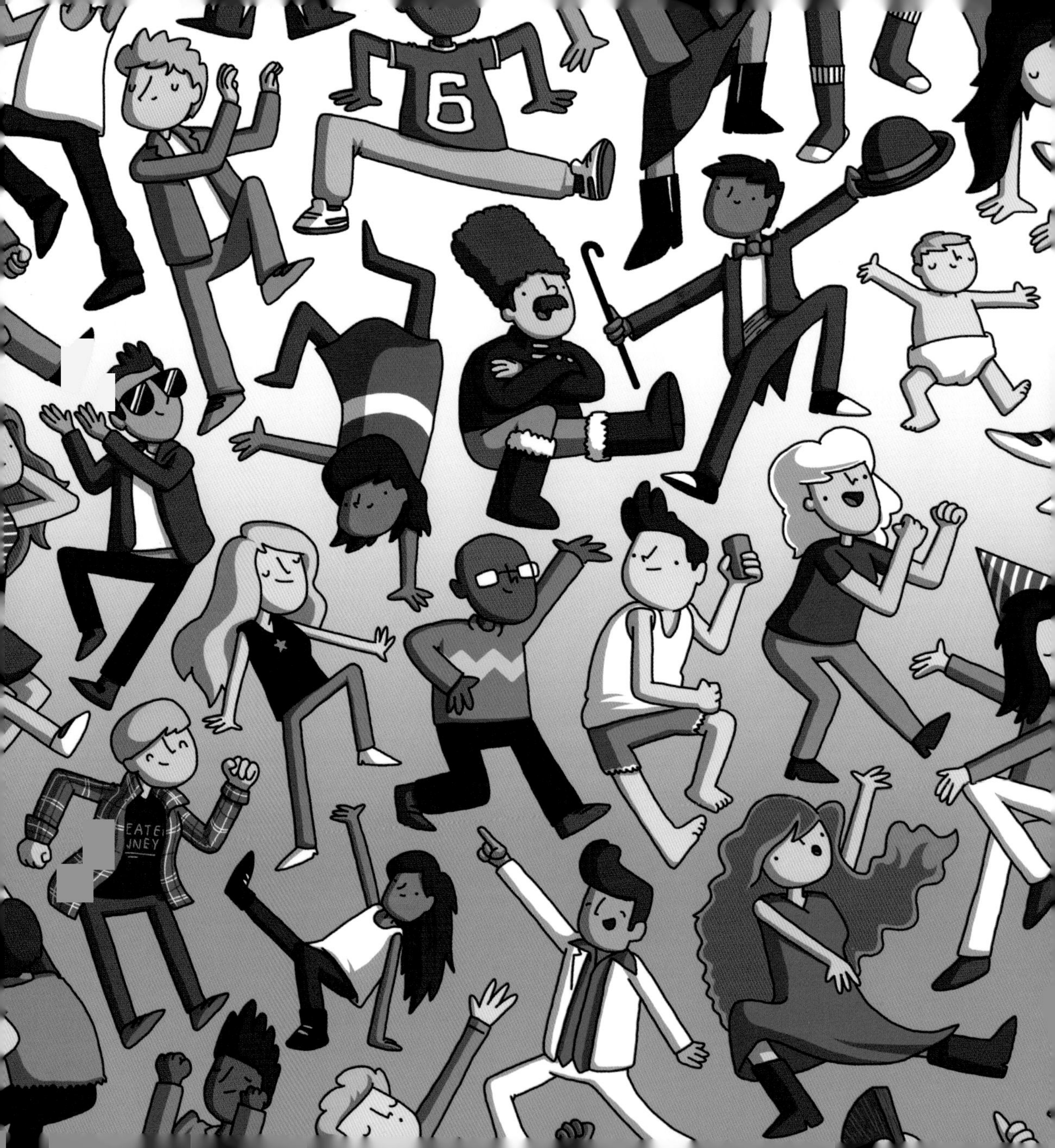
6

# DANCING

Do you love to bust-a-move? Get down? Well, so does the rest of the world! Some things are part of life all over the planet, and whether you live in Canada or Cambodia, dancing is absolutely one of them.

We've already read about bad dancers blaming wobbly floors and bad skirts for their terrible moves, but there are many positive expressions from all over the world about dancing, too!

## "DANCE BY YOURSELF, AND YOU CAN JUMP AS MUCH AS YOU WANT."

*"Μοναχός σου χόρευε, κι' όσο θέλεις πήδα."* **Greece**

The joys of freedom! Cooperation can be complicated, as anyone who's worked on a group project can tell you, but if you're going solo, you can do whatever you'd like. Nothing can stand in your way!

# "IT'S HARD TO DANCE IN BORROWED CLOTHES."

*"Person wey borrow cloth go party no dey dance too much."* **Nigeria**

When you're borrowing anything from a friend, it's important to be extra careful. You probably shouldn't use your most adventurous dance moves in borrowed clothes.

## "WITH MONEY, THE DOG DANCES."

*"Con el dinero, baila el perro."* **Mexico**

Money can make the unexpected happen. If you save up enough and invest in the best dog-trainers around, you can have a doggy dance squad in no time. Almost anything is possible when you've got the cash.

## "TRYING TO DANCE LIKE SOMEONE ELSE CAN HURT YOUR NECK."

*"Akka ebaluutti sirbaan morma nama jallisaa."* **Ethiopia**

Trying to change who you are to fit in with the crowd isn't a good idea; it's always best to be yourself.

"THE SPARROW, UNTIL 100 YEARS OLD, WILL NOT FORGET ITS DANCE."

"雀百まで踊り忘れず。"*Japan*

This Japanese saying is similar to the English phrase "a leopard can't change its spots."

## "A HUNGRY BEAR DOES NOT DANCE."

*"Νηστικό αρκούδι δεν χορεύει." **Greece***

This one is all about motivation—a bear won't dance if it's hungry, and most people need to get paid to work. The same phrase pops up in Bulgaria and Turkey too.

# BIRDS OF A FEATHER

## FLOCK TOGETHER

Family is all about sticking together through tough times and protecting one another. It's not just birds that stick together around the world though . . .

"Each sheep with its partner."

"Similar people are drawn to each other."

*Russia*

"A fisherman sees a fisherman from afar."

*Russia*  (again!)

"A goose is not a pig's friend."

*Czech Republic*

PLEASE...
THERE ARE
SO MANY...
OTHER...
FREE
BRANCHES...

"A crow sits next to a crow."

*France*

"Those who resemble, assemble."

*Pakistan*

"Old women are happy with old women."

*India*

FAMILY REUNION

"All thieves are cousins."

# LIKE FATHER, LIKE SON

GREAT AIM, SON!

It's internationally agreed upon that children often take after their parents, or as one saying goes in English, "the apple doesn't fall far from the tree." Here are some lovely non-fruit-based equivalents.

"Like river, like water." *(Andorra)*

"From such a stick, such a splinter." *(Spain)*

"The child of a frog is a frog." *(Japan)*

"The son of a fish knows how to swim."
*(Portugal)*

"Tigers do not have dogs for sons." *(China)*

"Dogs do not make cats." *(France)*

## "A BEETLE RECOGNIZES ANOTHER."

*"Aithníonn ciaróg ciaróg eile."* **Ireland**

This saying is all about family recognizing family and how it "takes one to know one." Beetles might all look alike to us, but to them, spotting the differences couldn't be easier.

## "THE CRAYFISH SIDES WITH THE CRAB."

*"가재는 게 편이라."* **South Korea**

Our similarities can be the foundations on which we build our relationships. While a crayfish and a crab are not direct family members, when you have so much in common, it's easy to strike up a friendship.

## "IN ITS MOTHER'S EYES, A MONKEY IS A GAZELLE."

"القرد في عين أمه غزالة" *Egypt, Saudi Arabia*

Parents see the best in their children. Even a humble monkey is as beautiful as a gazelle to its mother.
Gazelles are appreciated for their grace and beauty in the Middle East, so this is high praise.

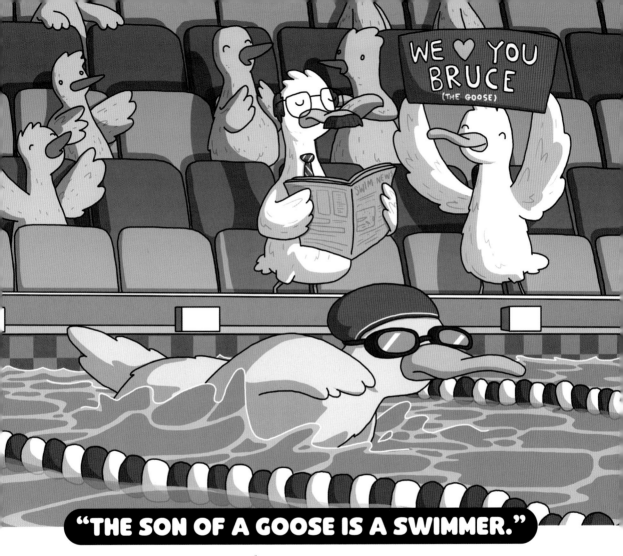

## "THE SON OF A GOOSE IS A SWIMMER."

"ابن الوزّ عوّام" *Egypt*

A nice goose-related companion phrase to "like father, like son." Some parental influences are unavoidable. If your dad is a goose, there's a good chance you'll have some goose-like qualities too.

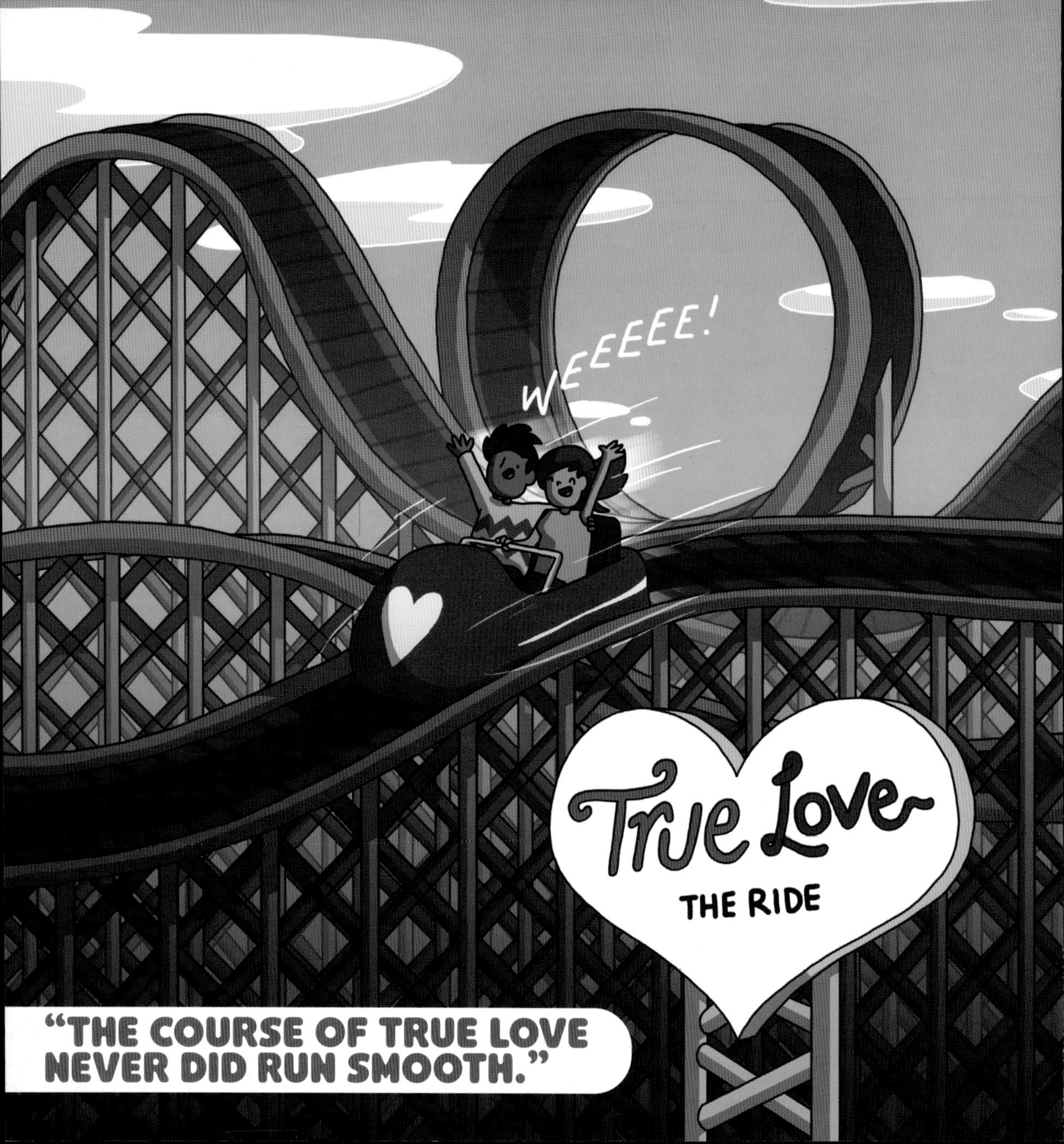
WEEEEEE!
True Love
THE RIDE
"THE COURSE OF TRUE LOVE NEVER DID RUN SMOOTH."

# LOVE

If you've ever heard a pop song, you might know a little bit about love. In fact, of the most popular songs of all time on the Billboard charts, 70% of them are love songs. Love is just that inspirational.

Shakespeare wrote, "The course of true love never did run smooth," and all relationships have their ups and downs, but from romantic love to the love between friends and family, it's the most powerful feeling there is. Every culture has its own way of talking about it, so if you want to write your own pop songs or just change up your love language, here are some phrases about love from around the world you can use for encouragement.

## "BEAUTIFUL MINDS FIND EACH OTHER."

*"Les beaux esprits se rencontrent."* **France**

Similar to "great minds think alike" but from a more romantic French point of view.

# "LOVE UNDERSTANDS ALL LANGUAGES."

*"Dragostea înţelege toate limbile."* **Romania**

While French might have a reputation as the most romantic language,
love is a language of its own, understood by all.

## "LOVE ME, LOVE MY DOG."

"爱屋及乌." *China*

When you love someone so much, you'll simply fall in love with the things they love.

# "THERE'S NO JAR SO HORRIBLE THAT IT CAN'T FIND A LID."

*"Il n'est si méchant pot qui ne trouve son couvercle."* **France**

There's someone for everyone out there; it's just a case of finding the right fit.

# BEAUTY IS IN THE EYE....

The sentiment "beauty is in the eye of the beholder" is known all over the world—beauty is up to you! It doesn't matter what you love, as long as you love it with all your heart.

"You're wearing glasses made for your eyes only."
(South Korea)

"Grass is sweet in the mouth of a goat."
(Iraq)

"A hippopotamus for a hippopotamus."
(Esperanto)

"Some like carrots while others prefer cabbage."
(China)

"Different flowers attract different eyes."
(China)

"DON'T THROW THE BABY OUT WITH THE BATHWATER."

# GOOD ADVICE

While so many proverbs try to express a lot of important significance on your life and outlook, some end up sounding like run-of-the-mill common sense—things that shouldn't really need saying at all. "Don't throw the baby out with the bathwater" is a perfect example. It's good advice in a situation where you want to hold on to something important, but it's especially useful to keep in mind when you're washing a baby.

This chapter looks at some more of those similarly useful/useless sayings from around the world. You can look to each phrase for a deeper meaning or just take it at face value as some sensible advice.

## "DON'T SAW OFF THE BRANCH YOU'RE SITTING ON."

*"Såga inte av den gren du sitter på."* **Sweden**

Similar to "don't bite the hand that feeds you," it's not advisable to upset the balance of anything you're benefitting from. In Italian, the saying goes, "don't spit in the dish you're eating from."

## "IF YOU HAVE TO CARRY A GOAT, DON'T WAIT FOR IT TO ROLL IN THE MUD."

*"Got we yu no se yu gɛt fɔ tot am, nɔ wet lɛ i rɔb pɔtɔ-pɔtɔ."* **Sierra Leone**

Leaving things to the last minute leads to unnecessary stress, so it's best not to delay.
As a Korean saying goes, "if you don't walk today, you'll have to run tomorrow."

## "DON'T TAKE TOO MUCH HAY ON YOUR PITCHFORK."

*"Neem nooit teveel hooi op je vork."* **The Netherlands**

This is about taking on more work or responsibility than you can handle, similar to "don't bite off more than you can chew." It might seem like a good idea, but you'll end up covered in hay.

## "IT'S BETTER TO BLOW LONGER THAN TO BURN YOUR MOUTH."

*"Het is beter om hard te blazen dan je mond te branden."* **The Netherlands**

It's foolish to jump into a situation without the proper preparation, especially when you might get hurt. "An ounce of prevention is worth a pound of cure," as they say, so be sensible with your soup.

## "HE WHO DIGS A PIT FOR OTHERS WILL FALL IN IT HIMSELF."

*"Cine sapă groapa altuia, cade singur în ea."* **Romania**

Originally a proverb from the Bible, this one is about how anyone who's hoping for the misfortune of others will most likely end up causing trouble for themselves.

## "YOU CAN'T BREAK A WALL WITH YOUR FOREHEAD."

*"Лбом сте́нку не расшибёшь." **Russia***

Some things are impossible to accomplish with brute force alone. Give what you're doing
some thought and have a better plan than smashing your head against it.

## "THE PILLOW IS THE BEST ADVISER."

*"Huvudkudden är bästa rådgivaren."* **Sweden**

When you're facing a tricky decision, sometimes it's best to just sleep on it. A rested mind is a sharper one, so have a little nap, and see what your pillow has to say.

## "LEAVE IT TO BATMAN."

*"Bahala na si Batman."* **The Philippines**

Proverbs aren't all dusty phrases from centuries ago—this one's pretty recent, only from the 1990s!
In times of struggle, sometimes all you can do is leave it to fate and/or the caped crusader.

# MEASURE TWICE, CUT ONCE

It's always better to plan ahead. When it comes to carpentry or sewing, you've got to make sure you measure your materials a few times *before* you make any cuts. Some places value preparation more than others, and that's reflected in the many versions of this phrase throughout the world.

Welcome to the Preparedness Olympics! Who will come out on top as the **most prepared**?

"Measure twice, cut once."
*(France, Germany, Italy, Sweden, Bulgaria Mexico, Greece . . . basically everywhere)*

"Measure three times, cut once."
*(The Netherlands)*
"Meet driemaal eer gij eens snijd."

## Bronze Medal

"Measure seven times, cut once."
*(Romania, Russia)*
*"De șapte ori măsoară, o dată taie."*

## Silver Medal

"Measure nine times, cut once."
*(Estonia, Lithuania)*
*"Üheksa korda mõõda, üks kord lõika."*

And congratulations to Malta,
taking home the Gold Medal!

"Measure
**one hundred times**,
cut once."
*(Malta)*
*"Qis mitt darba u aqta' darba."*

# TOO MANY COOKS

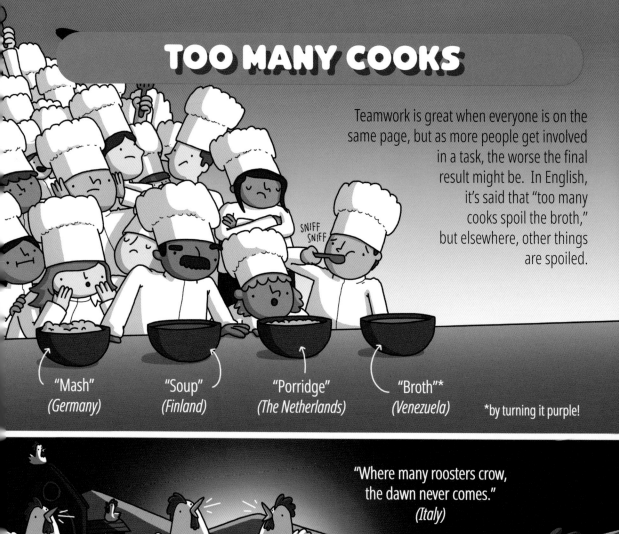

Teamwork is great when everyone is on the same page, but as more people get involved in a task, the worse the final result might be. In English, it's said that "too many cooks spoil the broth," but elsewhere, other things are spoiled.

SNIFF SNIFF

"Mash"
(Germany)

"Soup"
(Finland)

"Porridge"
(The Netherlands)

"Broth"*
(Venezuela)

*by turning it purple!

"Where many roosters crow,
the dawn never comes."
(Italy)

"Too many teachers will bring too many ghosts."*
(Vietnam)

*symbolic of stress

HNNNNGG!

"Too many rowers and the ship goes up the mountain."
(South Korea, Japan)

"Too many grandmothers spoil the child."
(Macedonia)

"Too many hands
on a plate cause
a lot of mess."
(Argentina)

"Three monks have
no water to drink."
(China)

WATER, ANYONE?
WE ARE DYING AFTER ALL...

OH NO,
I COULDN'T
IT'S YOURS

PLEASE, PLEASE,
DON'T BE SILLY.

"A dog with many masters will starve."
(Brazil)

"A boat with two captains would sink."
(Egypt)

HOW COULD YOU MISS THAT ICEBERG?!

I WAS BUSY STYLING MY BEARD, OK!

# DON'T COUNT YOUR CHICKENS

The English saying that you shouldn't "count your chickens before they've hatched" means it's not wise to make plans based on things that haven't happened yet. It dates back to at least 1570, and it's still in use today. How does the rest of the world interpret this idea? With fish, cats, and kimchi of course!

"Don't start licking
it up before it drops."
*(Finland)*

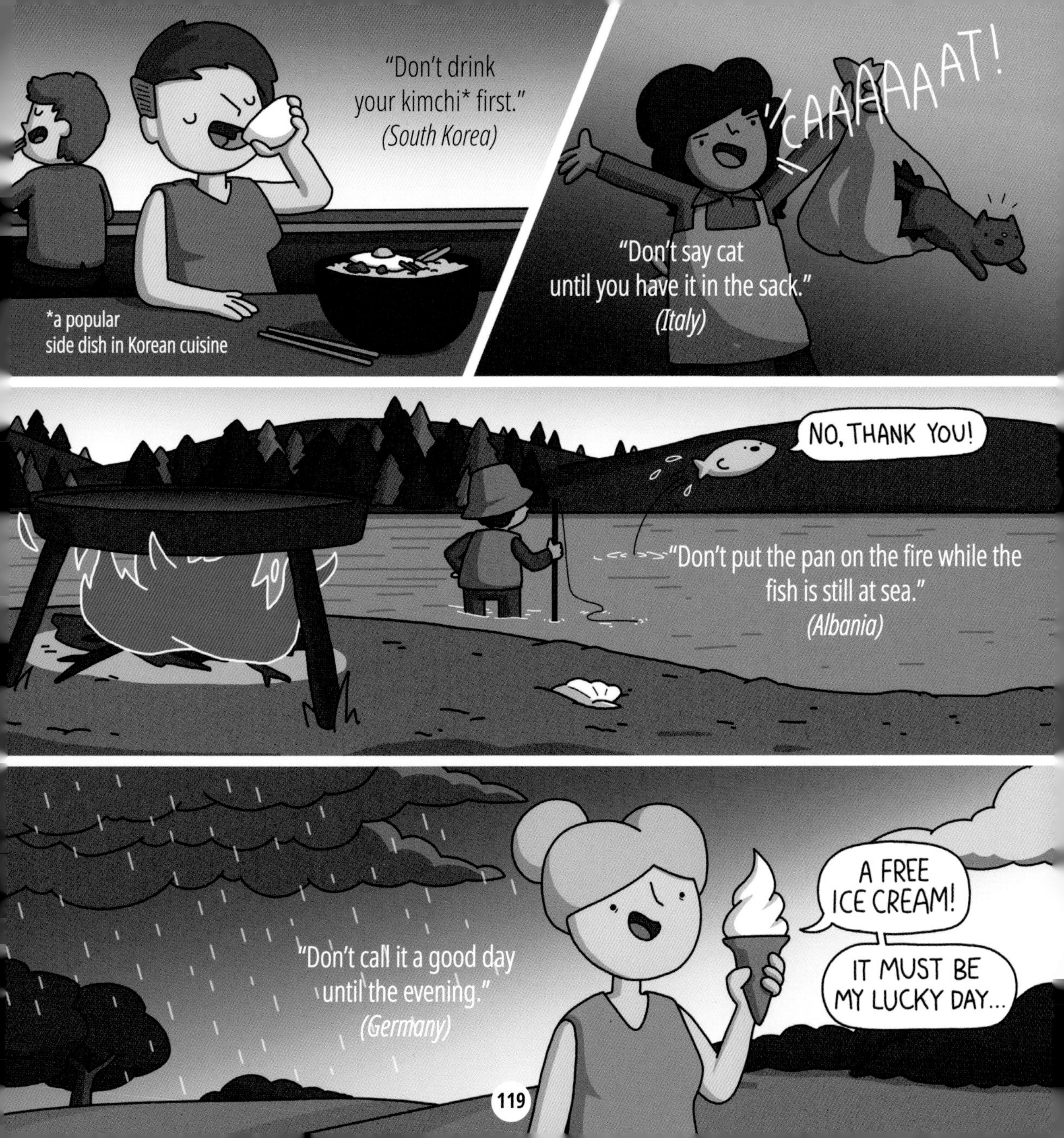
"Don't drink your kimchi* first."
(South Korea)
*a popular side dish in Korean cuisine
CAAAAAAAT!
"Don't say cat until you have it in the sack."
(Italy)
NO, THANK YOU!
"Don't put the pan on the fire while the fish is still at sea."
(Albania)
"Don't call it a good day until the evening."
(Germany)
A FREE ICE CREAM!
IT MUST BE MY LUCKY DAY...

# A BIRD IN THE HAND IS
# WORTH TWO IN THE BUSH

When faced with a choice between a smaller guaranteed reward and a potentially bigger but less certain one, this phrase suggests you stick with what you've got. Keep that bird well and truly in your hand, and leave those bush birds to their mysterious bushy business.

Possibly the oldest phrase in this book, "a sparrow in thy hand is better than a thousand sparrows flying," goes back to the ancient Aramaic proverbs in *The Words of Ahikar*, from 500 BC. The message is as true today as it was then: be satisfied with what you already have, and don't be greedy!

"A little fish is better than no fish."
*(Scotland)*

"Not getting what you chase and dropping what you carry."
(Malaysia)

"One is better than none."
(South Africa)

"An egg today is better than a hen tomorrow."
(Italy)

# OUT OF THE FRYING PAN
## INTO THE FIRE

*TSSSS!*
*TSS!*

SO LONG SUCKERS!

*TSSS!*

Dating back as far as 1490, this phrase is used when things go from bad to worse. Originally from a story about fish trying to jump to freedom to avoid being cooked and landing somewhere a little hotter, the same idea exists all over the world. No matter how bad things are, unfortunately, they might get worse!

OH, THIS IS MUCH WORSE.

"Escape a tiger, meet a crocodile."
*(Thailand)*

NICE TO MEET YOU!

AAAAHHH

"Out of the rain, and into the gutter."
*(Germany, Poland)*

NUTS.

"Ran from a wolf,
but into a bear."
*(Russia)*

"From the thickets
into the thornbushes."
*(Ireland)*

"Ran from the devil,
but into his dad."
*(Romania)*

"Escape a watermelon
rind to meet a
coconut shell."
*(Vietnam)*
*The toughest foods to get into!*

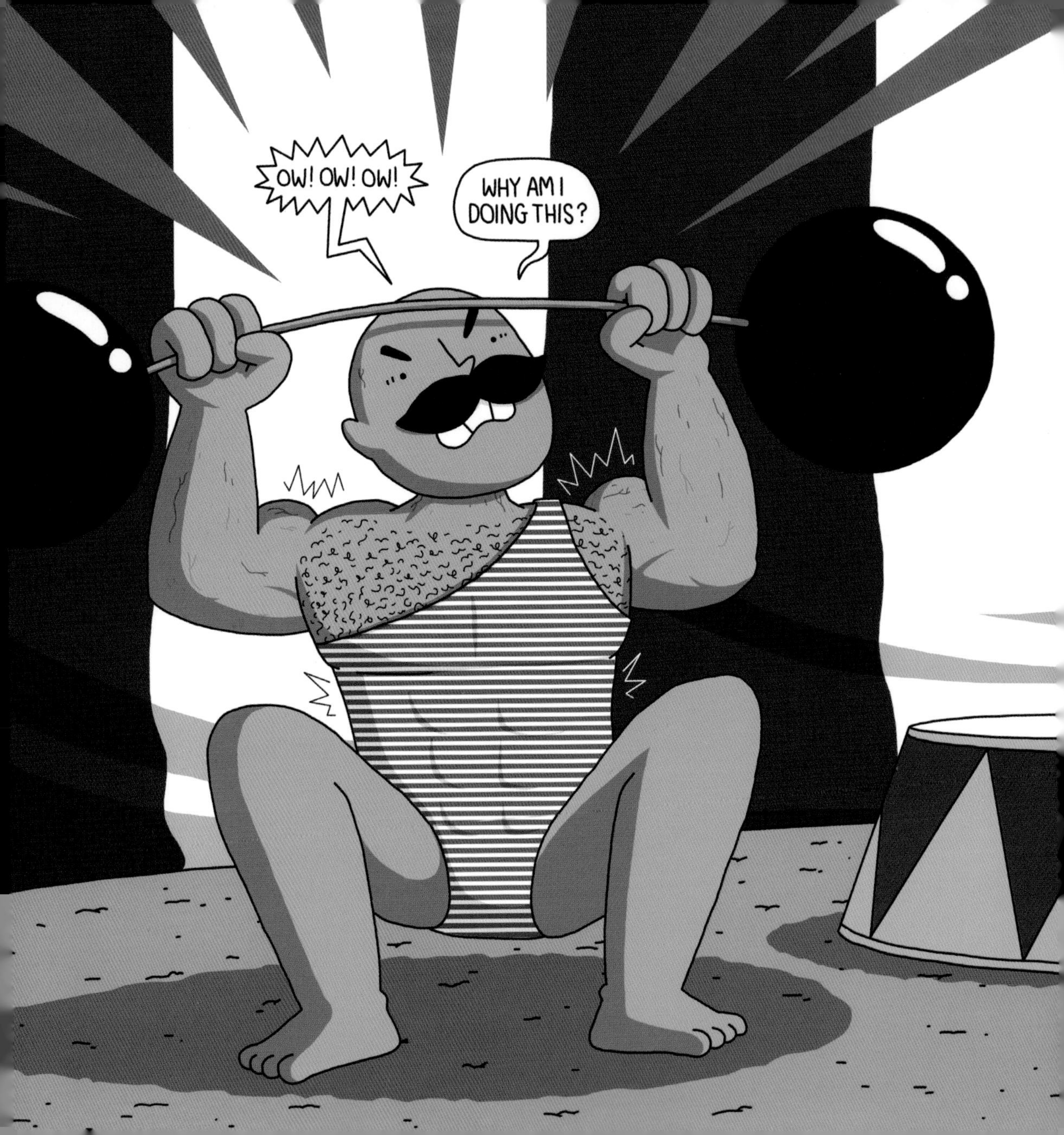
OW! OW! OW!
WHY AM I DOING THIS?

# NO PAIN, NO GAIN

From the physical strain required to obtain the world's beefiest physique to the intellectual stress of advanced astrophysics, reaching new heights isn't easy, and you've got to be tough to get to the top of your game.

Before this phrase became the motto of every gym on the planet, the first known usage of it was in Pirkei Avot 5:21, a Jewish text from the second century, stating "according to the pain is the gain." There must be something to this concept since it's stayed in popular usage for a few thousand years. While the English version deals with very general pain and a subsequent gain, the rest of the world gives some more specific examples of what you might have to overcome in order to get a brilliant reward.

# "IF YOU DON'T ENTER THE TIGER'S CAVE, YOU WILL NOT CATCH ITS CUB."

*"虎穴に入らずんば虎子を得ず." **Japan***

More tiger-related inspiration from Asia, this saying encourages you to ignore common sense and risk it all for a great reward. Used in China, Vietnam, and Korea too.

## "THE DOG THAT DOESN'T WALK DOESN'T FIND A BONE."

*"Perro que no camina, no encuentra hueso."* **Spain**

To achieve anything, you've got to put in the effort. Dogs that lay around in the sun will never get the Nobel Prize for bone-finding; that's for the pups that work for it.

## "NO ONE BECOMES A BISHOP WITHOUT A BEATING."

*"Enginn verður óbarinn biskup."* **Iceland**

It's a struggle to reach the top in any industry. But if this saying has any truth behind it, promotions in the Icelandic clergy sound a little tougher than most professions.

## "THERE ARE NO SWEETS WITHOUT FIRE."

*Egypt* "مافيش حلاوة من غير نار"

Just as batter needs an oven to become delicious cake, success, too, requires a bit of heat. When you're working hard, imagine yourself as a cake, rising to become the beautiful dessert you are!

## "THOSE WHO WANT YOGURT IN THE WINTER MUST CARRY A COW IN THEIR POCKET."

*"Zemheride yoğurt isteyen, cebinde bir inek taşır."* **Turkey**

This saying is about the sacrifices you need to make to get the finer things in life, whether that involves saving up for a new game system or breeding the world's tiniest cow for your yogurt needs.

## "NO ONE FINDS TREASURE WITHOUT TROUBLE."

*Iran* "نابرده رنج گنج میسر نمی شود"

It's not easy being a pirate, but the reward at the end of a long treasure hunt is worth the struggle.

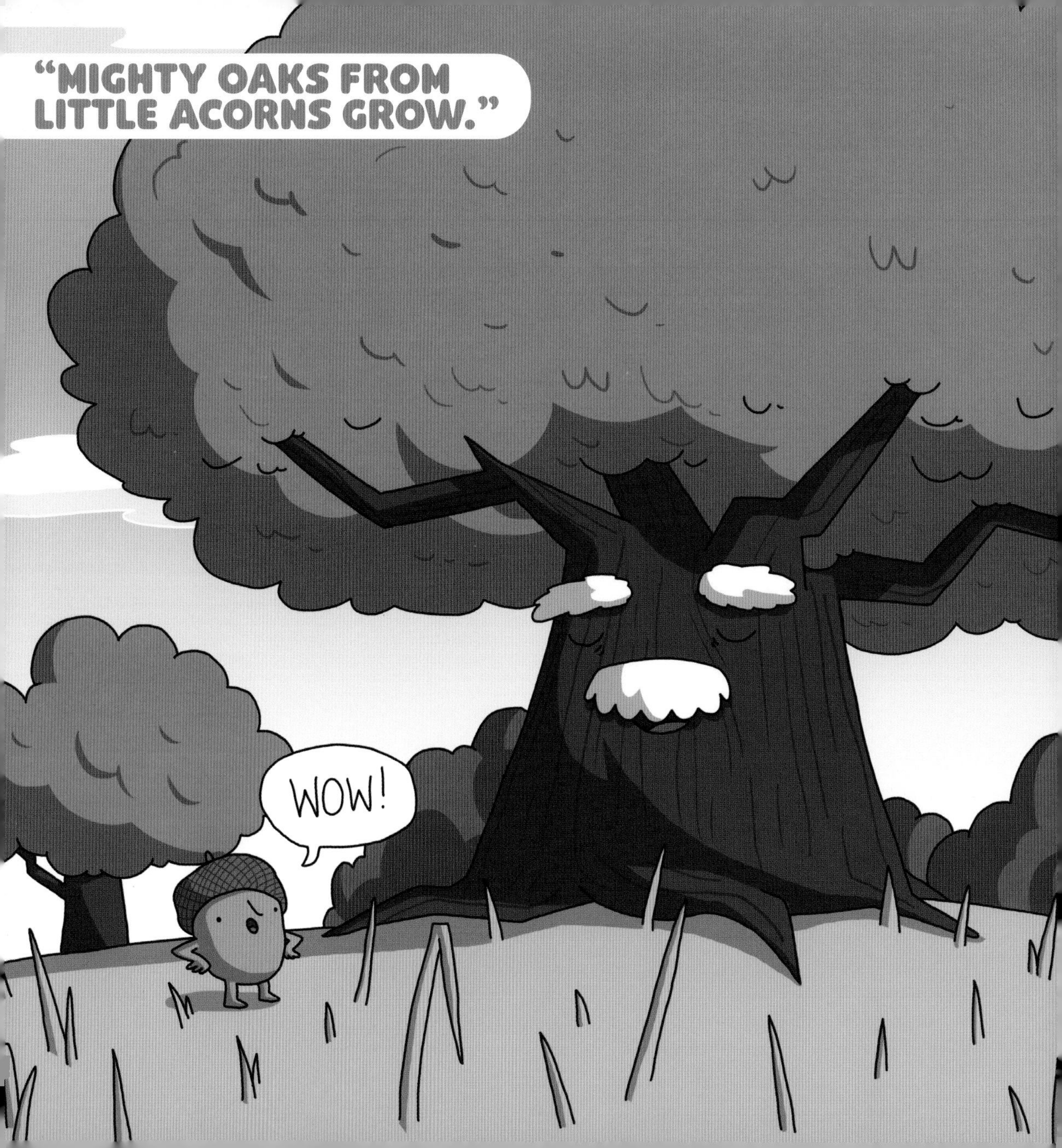
"MIGHTY OAKS FROM LITTLE ACORNS GROW."
WOW!

# PERSISTENCE

The secret to success is persistence and not giving up when things get tricky. There's a saying in English, "mighty oaks from little acorns grow," which can be taken to mean that greatness is achieved through many smaller actions that eventually pay off. Here are some international ways to say, "try, try again!"

## "THE FIRST PANCAKE IS ALWAYS A BLOB."

*"Пе́рвый блин всегда ко́мом."* **Russia**

Traditional Russian pancakes, called "blini," are eaten with sweet fillings like jam and honey, or sometimes caviar. The important thing is not to give up if the first one doesn't come out quite right.

## "FALL SEVEN TIMES, STAND UP EIGHT."

"七転び八起き."*Japan*

Defeats will inevitably come, but persistence is the key to eventual victory.

"EVEN THE BEST SCRIBE MAKES A BLOT."

*"El mejor escribano echa un borrón."* **Spain**

Pobody's nerfect, and we all make mistakes.

## "FORWARD SAID GRANDMA IN THE SNOW."

*"Eteenpäin sanoi mummo lumessa."* **Finland**

Whatever obstacle you're facing, it's possible to overcome it with the right attitude.

## "WILL IS A GOOD HORSE."

*"Ceffyl da yw ewyllys."* **Wales**

This "will" is actually willpower ("grym ewyllys") rather than a magnificent horse named Will. But a strong sense of determination will get you as far as lovely Will could.

## "EVEN DUST, WHEN PILED UP, WILL BECOME A MOUNTAIN."

"ちりもつもればやまとなる。" *Japan*

Small actions, over time, can amount to big achievements. Whether it's growing your dust collection or working hard towards another goal, every little bit helps.

# TWO HEADS ARE BETTER THAN ONE

The joys of teamwork! Instead of "too many cooks spoil the broth," these phrases are all about the successes we can find when we work together and help one another.

"Lifting together is better, even if it's just a piece of paper."
*(South Korea)*

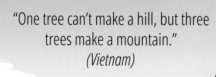

"One tree can't make a hill, but three trees make a mountain."
*(Vietnam)*

"Three people together
have more wisdom
than Monju."*
(Japan)

*an incredibly
wise Buddhist monk

"One hand
has nothing;
two hands
have sound."
(Turkey)

"Four eyes
see more
than two."
(Spain)

"You can't
lift two
watermelons
with one
hand."
(Iraq)

**141**

# YOU SNOOZE, YOU LOSE

Just as early birds catch the worm, a lot can be said for a timely start to the day. An old-timey English version of this sentiment goes "early to bed and early to rise, makes a man healthy, wealthy, and wise," so set your alarms early and go conquer that big old world in front of you!

- EMPLOYEE OF THE MONTH -

APRIL  MAY  JUNE  JULY  AUGU

"The early bird beats the hardworking person." *(The Philippines)*

"He who sleeps
doesn't catch any fish."
(Italy)

NUH-UH.

"The first up
the mountain can
sit where they want."
(China)

Les Nouvelles

WORLD SURRENDERS

"I SET MY
ALARM
EXTRA
EARLY!"

"The world
belongs
to those who
get up early."
(France)

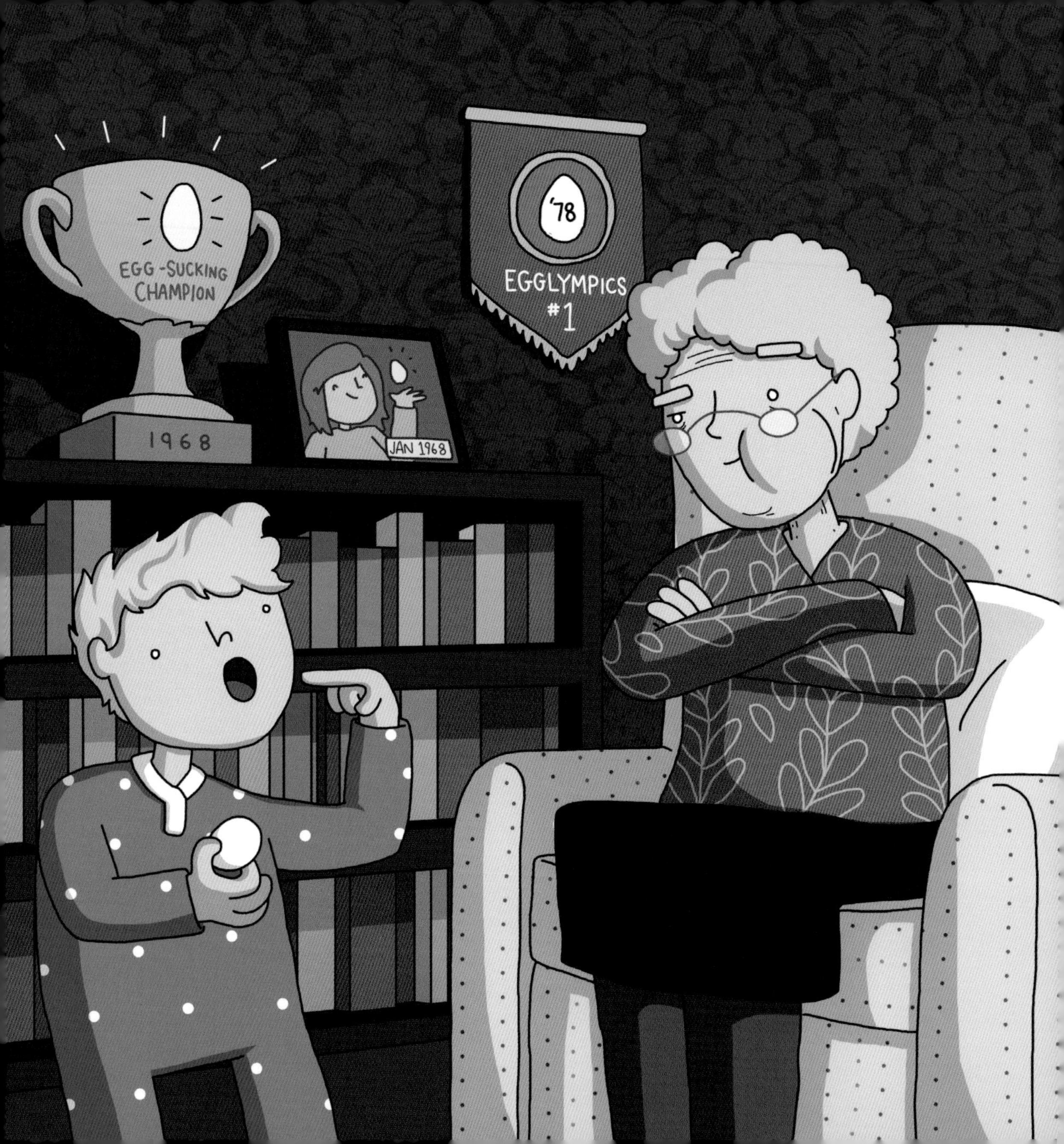
EGG-SUCKING CHAMPION
1968
JAN 1968
'78
EGGLYMPICS #1

# DON'T TEACH GRANDMA
# HOW TO SUCK EGGS

You don't get to old age without learning a thing or two about a thing or two, so thinking you can teach your elders how to do things might come across as a little disrespectful. Sucking eggs may not be so popular these days, but the phrase still shows up from time to time.

Originally from the work of Spanish author Francisco de Quevedo, translated into English in 1707, it caught on. While the literal meaning is no longer very relatable, the idea of some people thinking they know it all is always relevant. As these similar sayings show, it's not advisable to give advice to the experts.

## "YOU DON'T NEED TO TEACH A SNAKE HOW TO LIE DOWN."

*"Yu nɔ go tich snek haw fɔ ledɔn." **Sierra Leone***

Sierra Leone is home to a lot of snakes. In fact, hundreds of them took over a local police station once. Without any arms or legs, snakes don't need advice on how to lie down or apparently on how to trespass.

## "YOU CAN'T TEACH AN OLD MONKEY TO SMILE."

*"Ce n'est pas à un vieux singe qu'on apprend à faire la grimace."* **France**

Monkeys are the best at making funny faces. While you can't teach old dogs new tricks because they won't learn, you can't teach a monkey to smile because they're already an expert.

147

Dear Mr. A. Bird,

We are proud to present you with a licence to fly, certified by The International Board of Flying P...

Enjoy your time swooping aro...
loop-de-loops all o...
a barrel roll...
hig...

Ple...
and...
omb...

Yours sin...
Kim Planes...

# PILOT'S LICENCE

NAME    ANDREW BIRD.
ADDRESS    THE SKY.
DOB    06-12-99
ID NUMBER    24601
ADMINISTRATOR

APPROVED TO FLY

## "YOU DON'T NEED TO TEACH AN EAGLE TO FLY."

*"Neuč orla létat."* **Czech Republic**

Eagles are a symbol of strength in the Czech Republic—two of them are even featured on the Czech coat of arms—and with hunting speeds of up to 120mph, they certainly don't need any flying lessons.

## "LIKE TEACHING A CROCODILE TO SWIM."

*"สอนจระเข้ว่ายน้ำ." **Thailand***

Crocodiles were once fairly common around Thailand, and they turn up in a few Thai expressions. There's a folktale about a shape-shifting croc called Chalawan who can turn into a man, and a movie about him too!

# WHEN IN ROME, DO AS THE ROMANS DO

If you're traveling, it's great to absorb as much of the local culture as you can. After all, isn't appreciating different ways of life one of the reasons we travel? As much fun as it is for you to learn about a new place, it's also respectful to be mindful of local customs, so try to experience that local life!

"Enter the house, follow the customs; enter the river, follow the bends."
*(Vietnam)*

"Dance according to the music."
*(Brazil)*

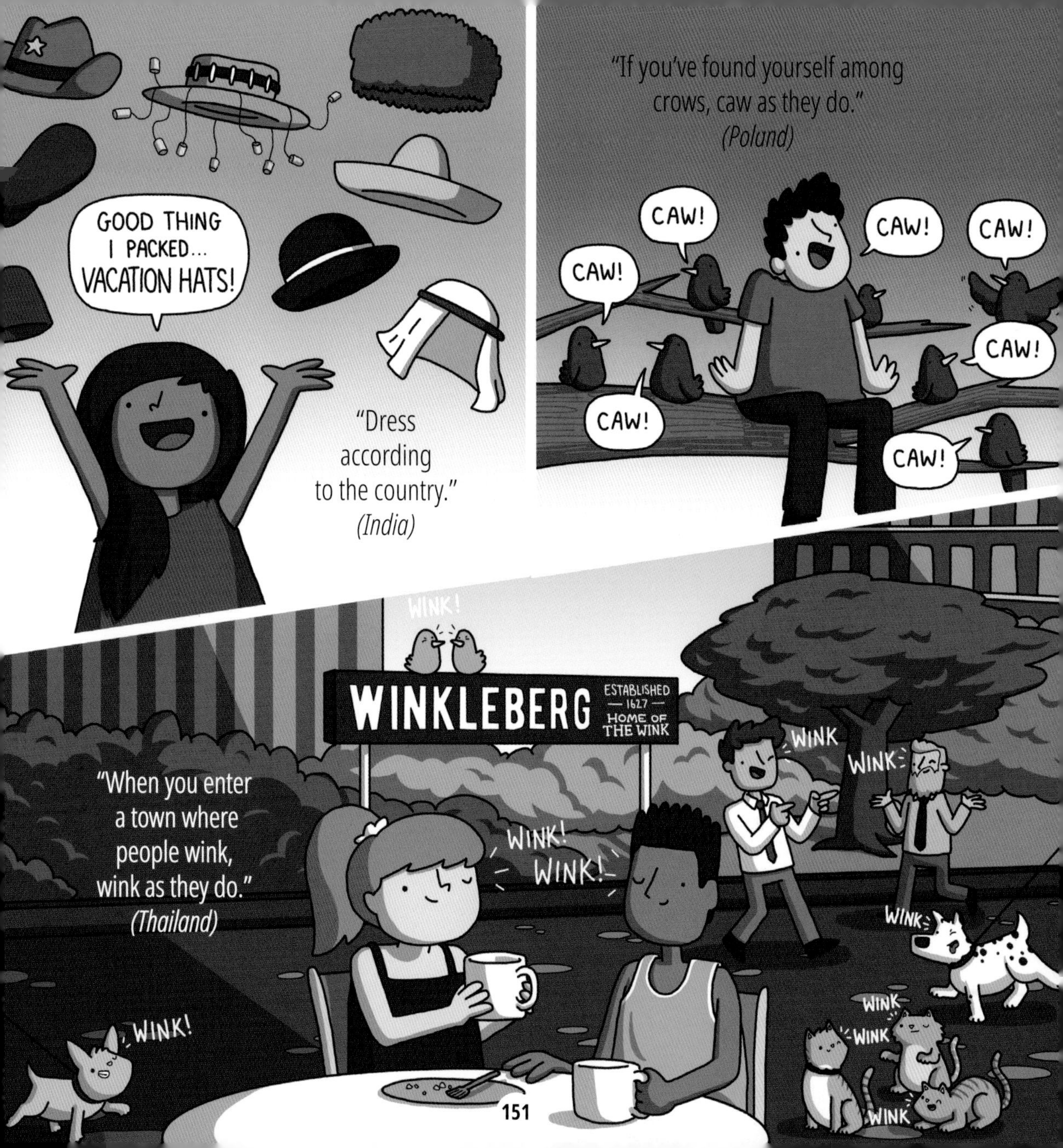
GOOD THING I PACKED... VACATION HATS!
"Dress according to the country."
(India)
"If you've found yourself among crows, caw as they do."
(Poland)
CAW!
CAW!
CAW!
CAW!
CAW!
CAW!
CAW!
WINK!
WINKLEBERG
ESTABLISHED — 1627 — HOME OF THE WINK
"When you enter a town where people wink, wink as they do."
(Thailand)
WINK! WINK!
WINK
WINK
WINK
WINK
WINK
WINK
WINK!

# ROME WASN'T
# BUILT IN A DAY

Speaking of Rome, it's a wonderful modern city but also one of the grand empires of antiquity; this saying is about the timescale of great achievements and how big tasks should never be rushed through.

Originally an old French proverb from the 1100s, this saying about Rome's greatness is known all around the world, but there are other local spins on the phrase showing hometown pride from Paris to Moscow to Carthage.

"Moscow wasn't built in a day."
*(Russia)*

"Paris wasn't built in a day."
*(France)*

"Carthage wasn't built in a day."
*(Esperanto)*

153

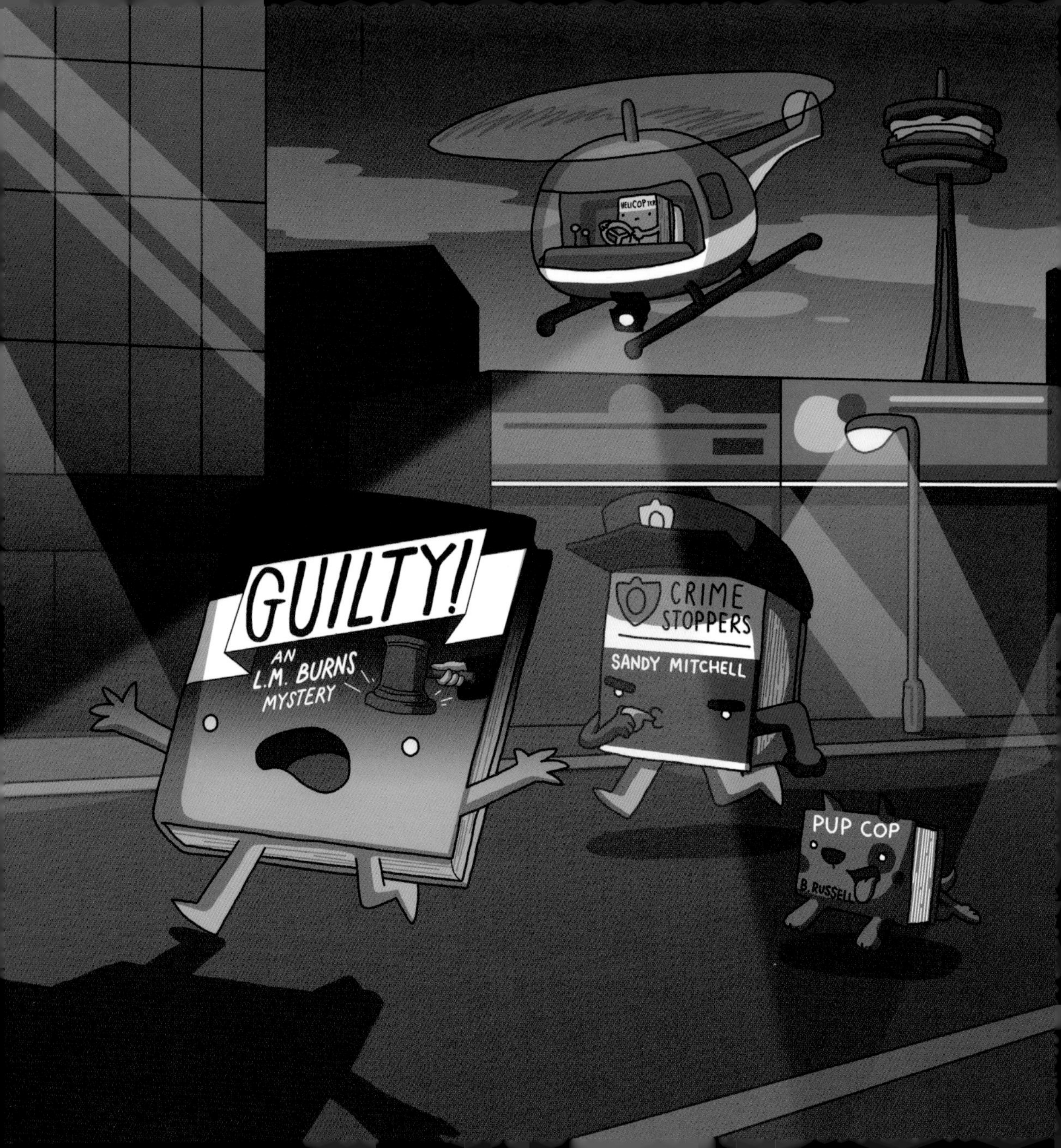
HELICOPTER
GUILTY!
AN L.M. BURNS MYSTERY
CRIME STOPPERS
SANDY MITCHELL
PUP COP
B. RUSSELL

# DON'T JUDGE A BOOK BY ITS COVER

Appearances can be deceiving. When you judge something based on your first impression, you could be missing the big picture, and what looks like a boring old book cover at first glance could turn out to be your new favorite.

At around 150 years old, this phrase is well-established in English, and the rest of the world has any other versions of this saying, featuring everything from monks to monkeys.

## "YOU SHOULDN'T JUDGE A DOG BY ITS FUR."

*"Man ska inte döma hunden efter håren."* **Sweden**

This is a popular saying around Scandinavia, which must mean their dog shows
are more snuggle fests than beauty contests. The way it should be!

## "CLOTHES DON'T MAKE THE MONK."

*"L'habit ne fait pas le moine."* **France**

Equivalent to "clothes don't make the man" in English, this one is used in
Italy and Spain, as well as reaching some parts of India too.

# "THE TASTE OF THE SAUCE IS BETTER THAN THE TASTE OF THE BOWL."

*"뚝배기보다 장맛이 좋다." **South Korea***

Korean cuisine uses quite a lot of sauce and a fair few bowls, and one definitely tastes a lot better than the other. A similar phrase can be found in Hebrew: "don't look at the jug, but what's inside it."

# "A NICE FIG IS OFTEN FULL OF WORMS."

*"Ikhiwane elihle ligcwala izibungu."* **South Africa**

They say beauty is only skin deep, and if your fig's full of worms, that sounds about right.
Fig fact: Some figs do actually contain fig wasps that help the fig reproduce.

## "EVEN WHEN A MONKEY IS DRESSED IN SILK, IT'S STILL A MONKEY."

*"Aunque la mona se vista de seda, mona se queda."* **Spain**

This phrase is about dressing things up as more valuable than they are.

## "UNDER THE SHEIKH'S HAT IS A MONKEY."

"تحت العمّة قرد" *Egypt*

In Arabic culture, sheikhs are members of high society, and you can't get much lower than a monkey. Similar silk-wearing Spanish monkeys, you can't always trust the outer packaging.

"EVERY CLOUD HAS A SILVER LINING."

# THE NATURAL WORLD

Whether it's green grass or hard rocks, beautiful rain or bad apples, the natural world affects us all. The weather, for example, is a popular topic of conversation in every country, so it comes as no surprise that weather-themed phrases work their way into most languages, often reflecting each countries climate. Warmer countries tend to talk more about the heat, while wetter places go on about the amount of rain. But as they say, "every cloud has a silver lining," and from bad weather, great phrases are born.

# "HOW BEAUTIFUL IT IS TO SEE THE RAIN AND NOT GET WET."

*"Qué bonito es ver la lluvia y no mojarse."* **Spain**

This lovely saying is actually quite sassy. It's used when people criticize
something without knowing how much effort has gone into it.

## "THE MOUNTAIN IS NOT AFRAID OF SNOW."

*"Το βουνό τα χιόνια δε φοβάται."* **Greece**

This phrase is perfect for those times when nothing is going your way. Be like Mount Olympus weathering the storm, and you'll still be standing after the bad times have passed.

## "IF THE WORLD FLOODED, IT WOULDN'T MATTER TO A DUCK."

*"Dünyayı sel bassa ördeğe vız gelir."* **Turkey**

Similar to "like water off a duck's back," but more extreme.
What might be a big problem to some, doesn't affect others at all.

# "THE SUN WILL NOT STAY BEHIND A CLOUD."

"Արևն ամպի տակ չի մնայ." *Armenia*

A saying similar to "the truth will out" in English, this means that secrets will always be revealed eventually. The answer may be clouded for now, but soon the truth will shine.

# "EVEN INTO A MOUSE HOLE, THE SUN SHINES."

"쥐구멍에도 볕들 날 있다." *South Korea*

Nothing is as bad as it seems, and even a dark and cramped mouse hole sees a little bit of sun from time to time. No matter how bad your situation, something good is just over the horizon.

## "DON'T GROW TOO HIGH LEST A STORM KNOCK YOU OVER."

"অতিবাড় বড়ো নাকো ঝড়ে পড়ে যাবে।" *India*

"Don't get too big for your britches" is a similar American-English phrase. Overconfidence in your abilities might lead to a setback if you're not careful.

# IT'S RAINING CATS & DOGS

This is one of those phrases that's so old, no one can say for sure where it originally came from, but in times of heavy rain, it's clearly common to feel that maybe there's more than just water falling from the sky. Here's how the world describes those wet, wet days. They say it's raining:

"cats and dogs" (English)

"chair legs" (Greece)

"barrels and casks" (Andorra)

"lizards and snakes" (Brazil)

"husbands" (Colombia)

"ropes" (France)

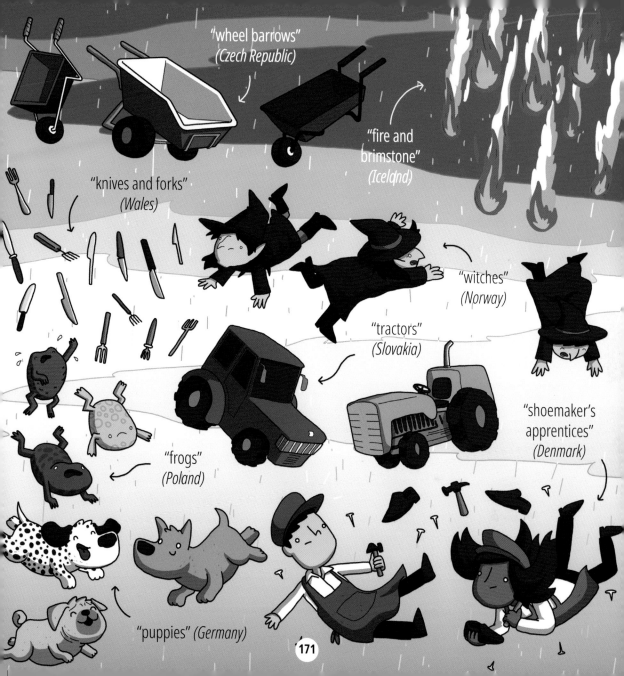

"wheel barrows" (Czech Republic)

"fire and brimstone" (Iceland)

"knives and forks" (Wales)

"witches" (Norway)

"tractors" (Slovakia)

"shoemaker's apprentices" (Denmark)

"frogs" (Poland)

"puppies" (Germany)

# THE GRASS IS GREENER
# ON THE OTHER SIDE

There are pros and cons in everyone's lives, and it's great to strive for the best, but envying those who seem to have it better can be shortsighted. Like a sheep wanting another's grassy field, or an English author jealous of more exciting foreign sayings, it's often best to focus on what you have.

"The distant drum sounds pleasant."
(India)

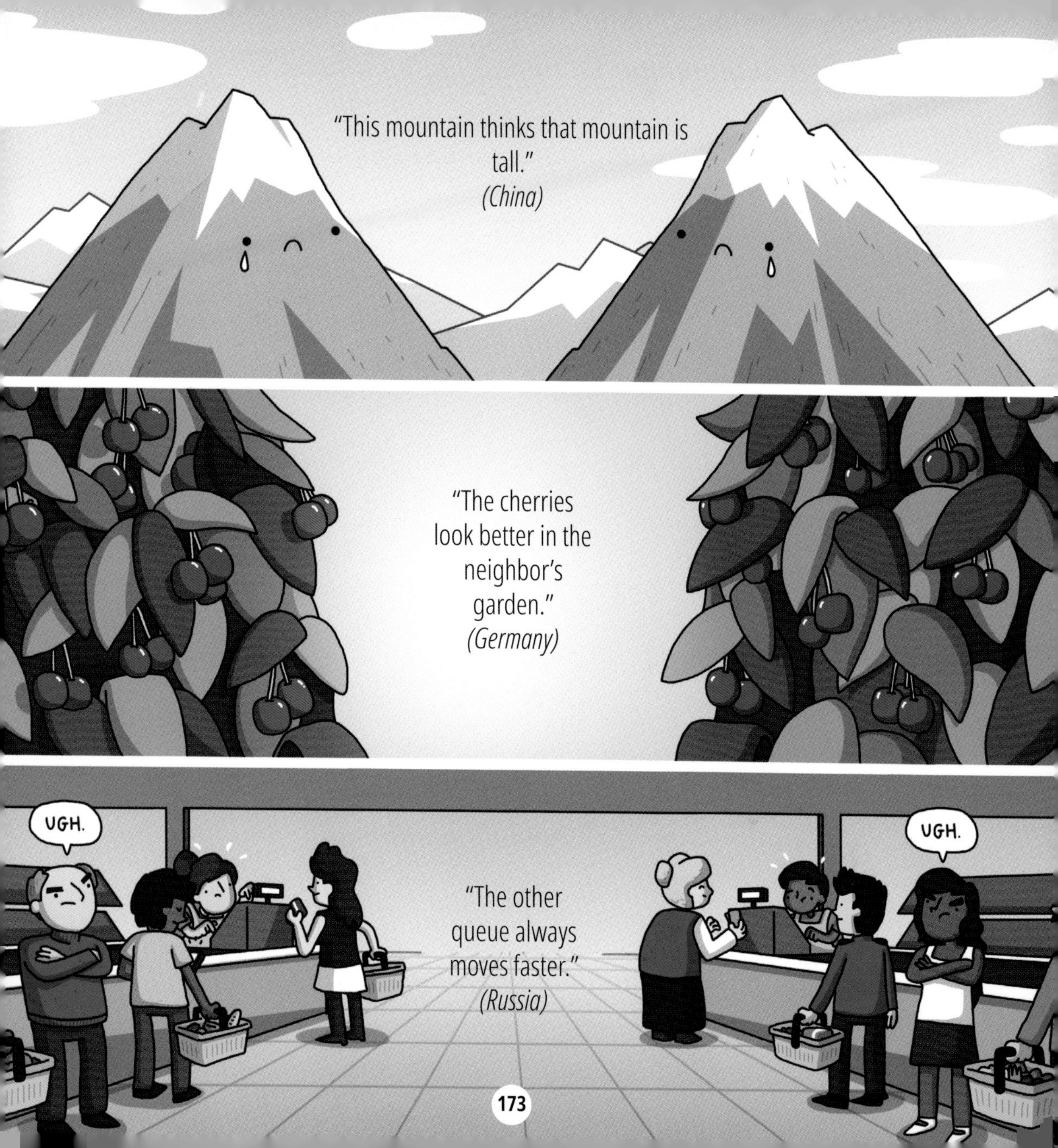
"This mountain thinks that mountain is tall."
(China)
"The cherries look better in the neighbor's garden."
(Germany)
UGH.
"The other queue always moves faster."
(Russia)
UGH.

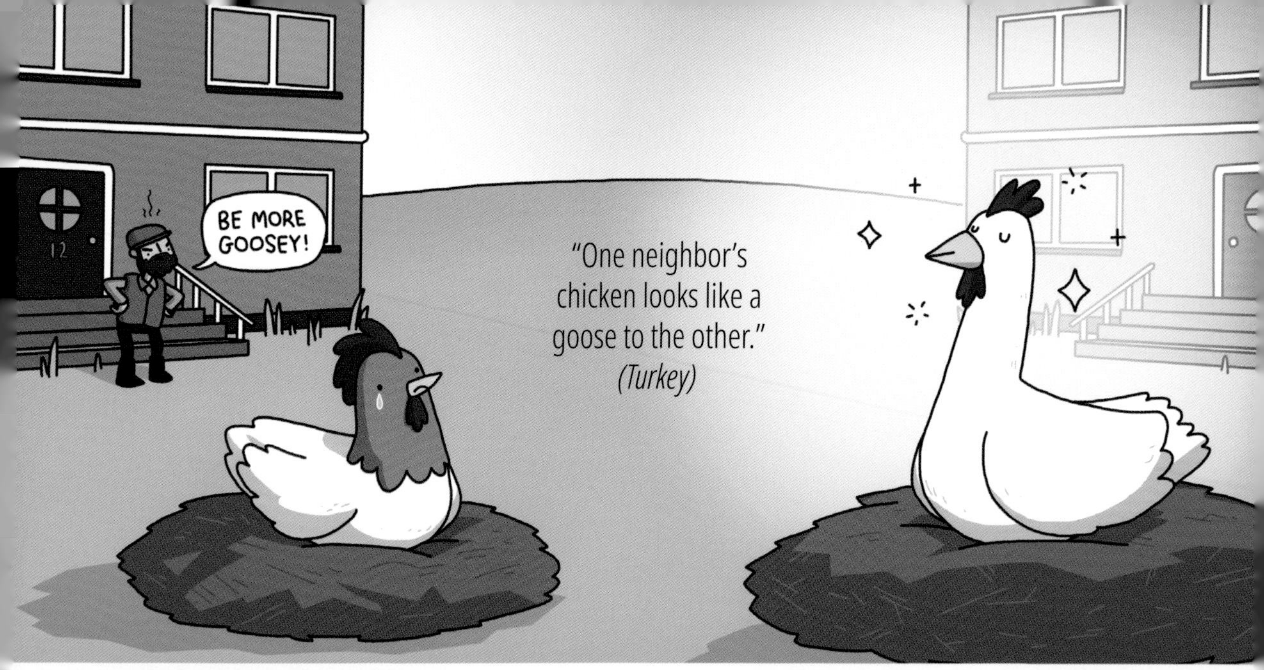
BE MORE GOOSEY!
12

"One neighbor's chicken looks like a goose to the other."
*(Turkey)*

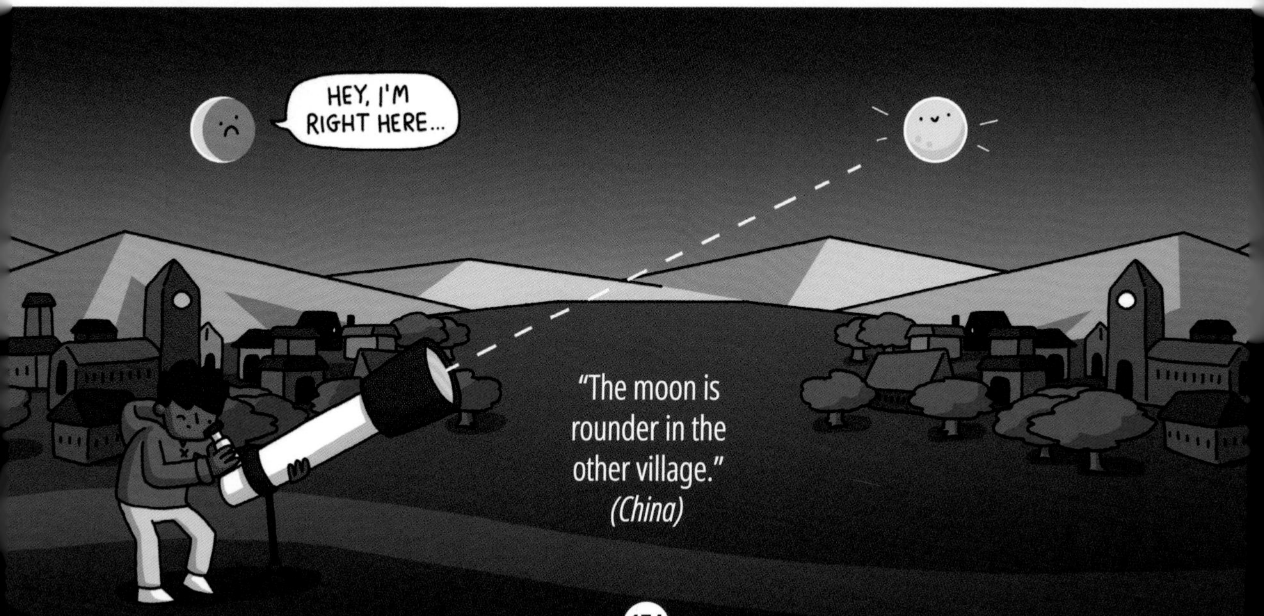
HEY, I'M RIGHT HERE...

"The moon is rounder in the other village."
*(China)*

"The desire of the duck
is the loch where she is not."
(Scotland)

"Other people's
rice cakes look bigger."
(South Korea)

LOCH SHIEL

LOCH TREIG

# A ROCK & A HARD PLACE

The struggle to choose between two terrible options is a problem that most of us have faced at one time or another. The English version of this phrase dates back to early 1900s America with the decision between unsafe work in the mines (choosing "a rock") and the unemployment ("a hard place"), and versions of this sentiment exist worldwide.

"Between a rock and a hard place."
*(English)*

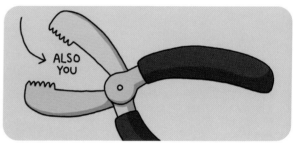

"Between the pliers' jaws."
*(Egypt)*

"Between the anvil and the hammer."
*(Italy)*

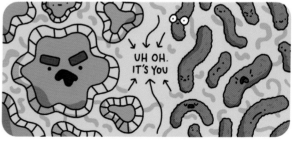

"Between plague and cholera."
*(Sweden)*

"Between the tree and the bark."
*(France)*

"A flea, between fingernails."
*(Faroe Islands)*

"Between the sword and a wall."
*(Spain)*

"Between two boards."
*(Japan)*

"Between two fires."
*(Iceland)*

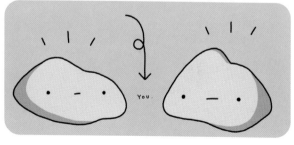

"Between two stones."
*(Armenia)*

"HAVE YOUR CAKE AND EAT IT TOO."

# FOOD & DRINK

Whether you're a couch potato, a top banana, cool as a cucumber, or someone's cup of tea, food phrases come up a lot more often than you might think.

When traveling around the world, one of the most amazing—and delicious—differences between places is the cuisine. Variations in local foods seep into language and food related expressions around the globe. There's a whole world of food and fun phrases that go along with it.

# A FEW BAD APPLES

"A few bad apples spoil the whole barrel" is a phrase that suggests the good reputation of a group can be spoiled by a few bad actors within it. While the idea has been interpreted in different ways in different languages, it's proven to be a timeless concept, with the English version dating back as far as the thirteenth century, and still used regularly to this day.

"A few bad apples spoil
the whole barrel."
(English)

"One mouse poop
spoils the porridge."
(China)

"One worm upsets
a pot of soup."
(Vietnam)

"One rotten fish
pollutes the whole pond."
(India)

"One mangy sheep
infects the whole flock."
(Czech Republic)

"One bad coconut makes
the good ones bad."
(Kenya)

## "EVERY VEGETABLE HAS ITS TIME."

*"Всякому óвощу своё врéмя."* **Russia**

Just as we find our successes at different times in life, vegetables are all waiting for that day of peak ripeness. This is a nice alternative to "every dog has its day" that makes a bit more sense.

# "THERE'S A BAD POTATO IN EVERY SACK."

*"Y mae taten ddrwg ym mhob sach."* **Wales**

In every group of people, they say one will let the others down, like the weakest link in the chain. Bad apples, bad coconuts, and now bad potatoes; it's interesting how some foods cause such trouble.

## "A DUCK COMES ALONG CARRYING A LEEK ON ITS BACK."

*"かもがねぎをしょってくる." Japan*

To make duck soup, you need a leek and some duck, so finding both in the same spot would be ideal! This phrase is for any lucky situations when the stars seem to align.

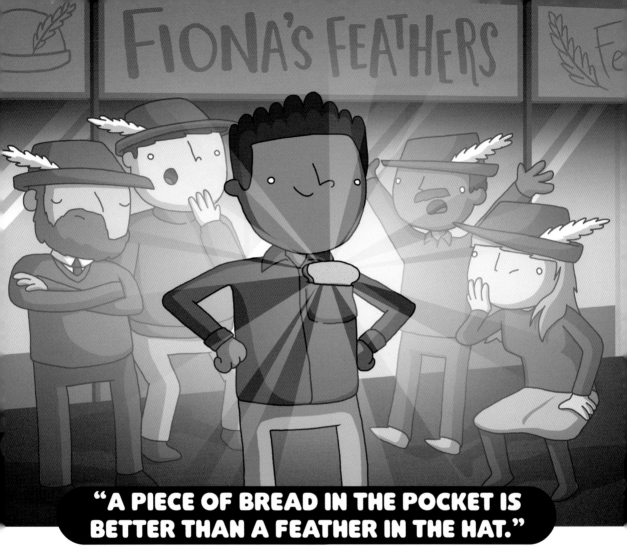

## "A PIECE OF BREAD IN THE POCKET IS BETTER THAN A FEATHER IN THE HAT."

*"En bit bröd i fickan är bättre än en fjäder i hatten."* **Sweden**

According to this phrase, it's much more important to have the essentials like food and shelter than it is to have the latest fashionable fad. Make sure you prioritize the important things in life.

# SELLING LIKE HOTCAKES

In cold weather, hotcakes are a great thing to eat, and if you're selling them, they'll be gone before you know it. In warmer climates, however, cakes are not always the bestsellers, with other items off the shelves first.

"Selling like sweet rolls."
*(The Netherlands)*

"Selling like cheese and bread."
*(Turkey)*

"Selling like sugar."
*(Hungary)*

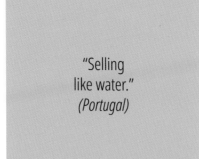

"Selling
like water."
(Portugal)

"Selling like
butter."
(Sweden)

"Selling like
hot bread."
(Spain, Denmark)

"Selling like
fresh shrimp."
(Vietnam)

# THERE'S NO USE CRYING OVER SPILT MILK

When the irreversible has happened, there is no sense dwelling on it. What's done is done, and as much as you want it, that milk can't be salvaged. Spilt milk has been the go-to example of a lost cause in English since at least 1659 (though in a much fancier old-timey way: "no weeping for shed milk").

"Crying doesn't help at the fair."
(Finland)

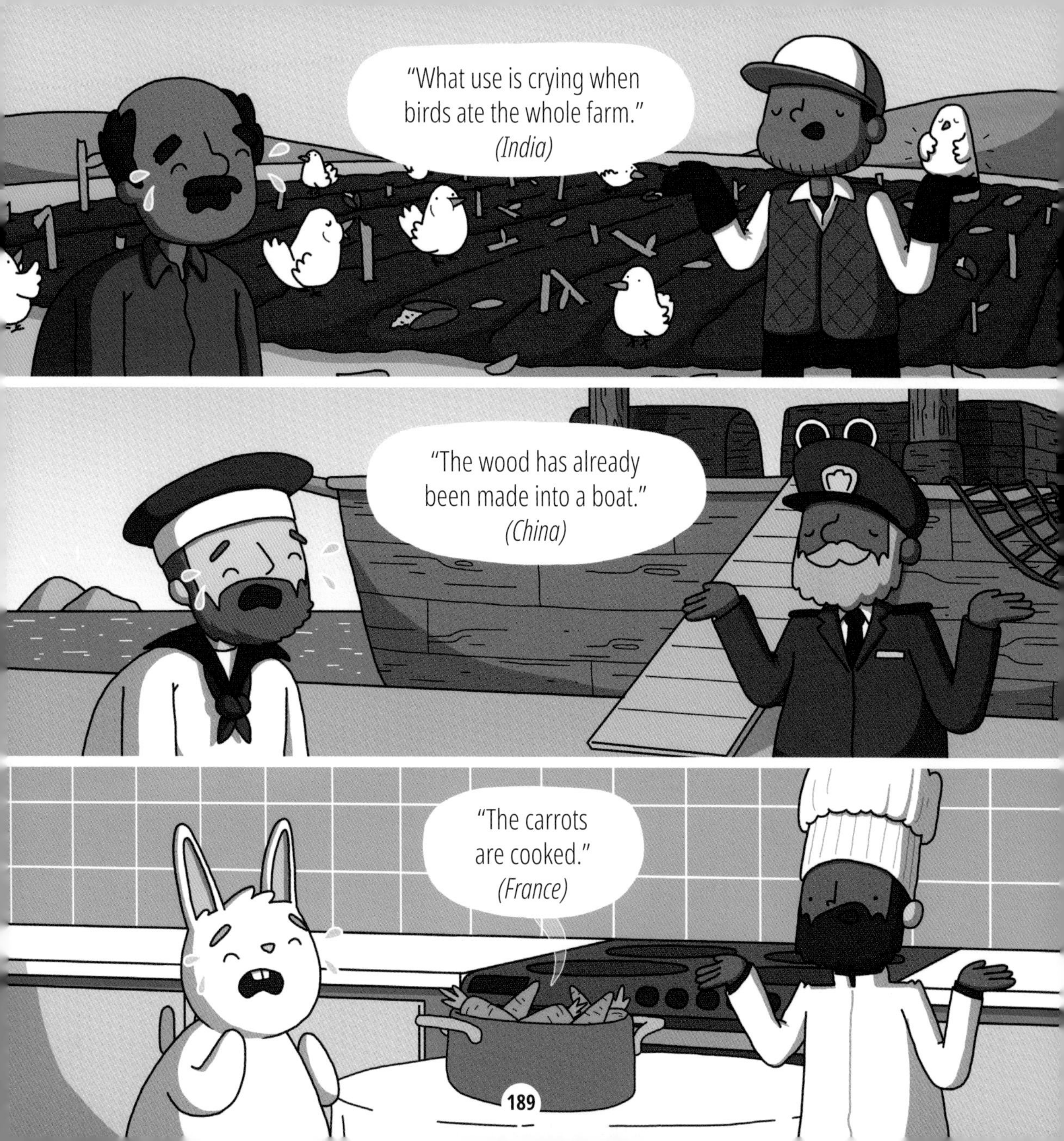
"What use is crying when birds ate the whole farm."
(India)
"The wood has already been made into a boat."
(China)
"The carrots are cooked."
(France)

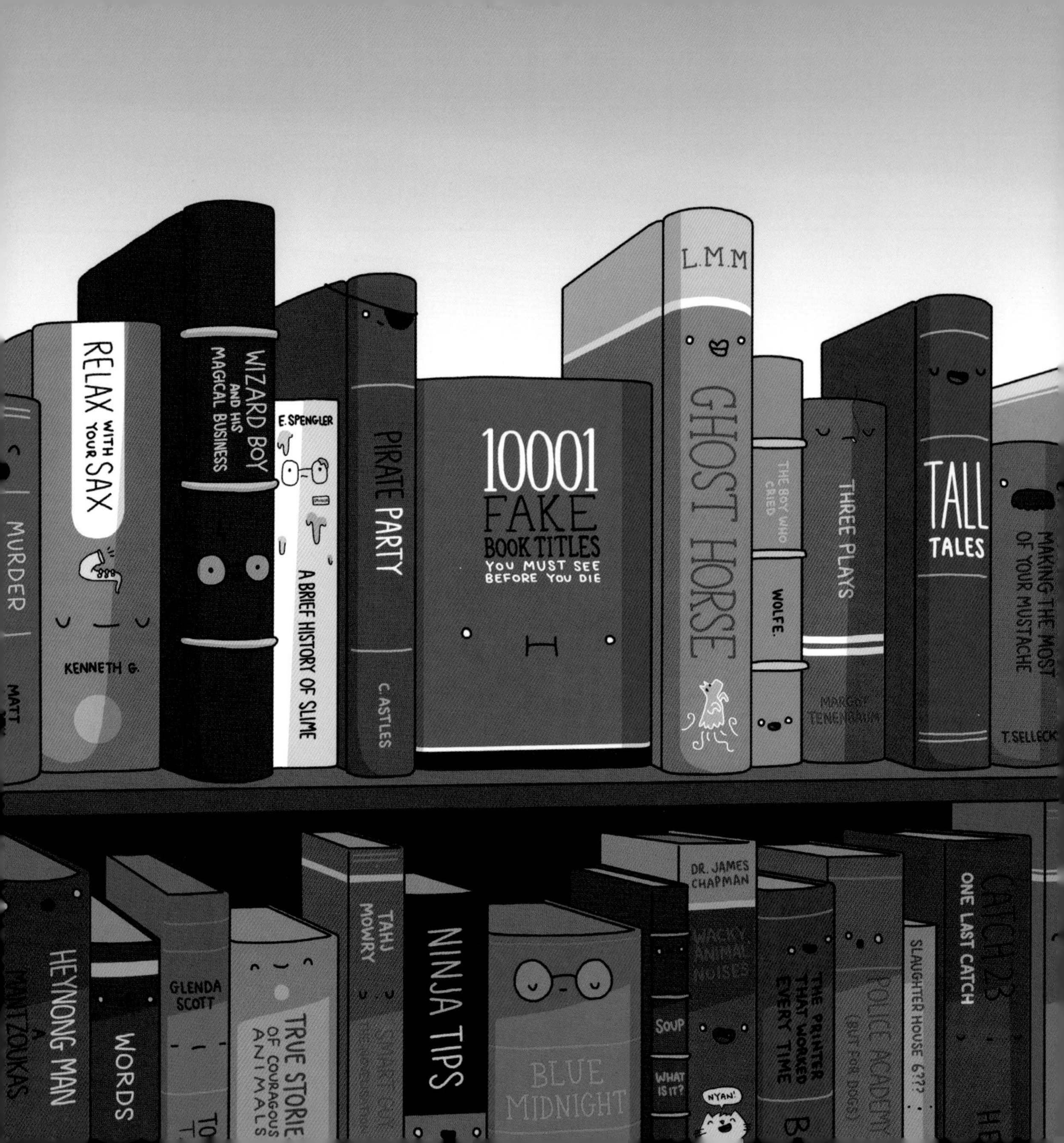
MURDER
MATT
RELAX WITH YOUR SAX
KENNETH G.
WIZARD BOY AND HIS MAGICAL BUSINESS
E. SPENGLER
A BRIEF HISTORY OF SLIME
PIRATE PARTY
C. ASTLES
10001 FAKE BOOK TITLES YOU MUST SEE BEFORE YOU DIE
L.M.M
GHOST HORSE
THE BOY WHO CRIED
WOLFE.
THREE PLAYS
MARGOT TENENBAUM
TALL TALES
MAKING THE MOST OF YOUR MUSTACHE
T. SELLECK
HEYNONG MAN
MANTZOUKAS
WORDS
GLENDA SCOTT
TRUE STORIES OF COURAGEOUS ANIMALS
TAHJ MOWRY
NINJA TIPS
BLUE MIDNIGHT
SOUP
WHAT IS IT?
DR. JAMES CHAPMAN
WACKY ANIMAL NOISES
NYAN!
THE PRINTER THAT WORKED EVERY TIME
POLICE ACADEMY (BUT FOR DOGS)
SLAUGHTER HOUSE 6???
ONE LAST CATCH
CATCH 23

# BOOKS

It's undeniable—books are amazing! Why else would you be reading one right now? Whether you're learning about the world around you or getting a glimpse of somewhere far away, reading makes anything possible.

There aren't too many English expressions about books themselves (aside from not judging them by their covers), but other cultures can't get enough of them. The phrases in this section perfectly capture how important and valuable reading can be and make a compelling case for why books should really replace dogs as "man's best friend." Sorry, dogs.

## "A GOOD BOOK IS A GOOD FRIEND."

*"好书如挚友." China*

Much like your best buds, a good story will stick with you and meaningfully impact your life. They're some of the greatest companions you could ever have.

## "A BOOK IS LIKE A GARDEN CARRIED IN THE POCKET."

*"书是随时携带的花园." China*

Gardens and books both need attention to fulfill their potential, and great beauty can be found in each of them. Don't get them mixed up though—no one needs pockets full of soil.

# "A BOOK HOLDS A HOUSE OF GOLD."

"书中自有黄金屋." *China*

Sure, books are full of beauty and whatever, but this phrase is all about the money! It suggests that if you can become well-read, you'll rise to the top—maybe with your own solid gold house.

## "THERE'S NO THIEF WORSE THAN A BAD BOOK."

*"Non c'è peggior ladro di un libro cattivo."* **Italy**

Not all books are great, and as time is the most valuable thing we have, it's a real shame to waste it reading something you don't like.

# IT'S ALL GREEK TO ME

Some of the sayings in this book may have left you scratching your head in confusion, saying "it's all Greek to me." But what would a Greek person say when *they're* confused? It turns out most languages reference another when they're baffled—an international chain of bewilderment!

In Greek,* some say, "am I speaking **Turkish**?"
*in Cyprus

In Turkish, "I'm **French** to this."

In French, they say, "it's **Hebrew**."

In Hebrew, "It's **Chinese** to me."
also used in French, Greek, and Spanish

And in Chinese, they say, "it's **ghost script**."

Boo!

And ghosts have yet to comment.

Woooo.o..

# APPENDIX

**"The world is your oyster."**
**ES** *El mundo es su lienzo*
**DE** *Die Welt liegt einem zu Füßen*
**RU** *Весь мир к твоим услугам*
**AM** *Աշխարհը խաղալիկ ինք մեջը շրջիկ*
**PL** *Świat stoi przed kimś otworem*
**JP** この世は思いのまま

**"When the cat's away . . . "**
**FI** *Kun kissa on poissa, hiiret hyppivät pöydällä*
**FR** *Quand le chat n'est pas là, les souris dansent*
**BR** *Quando o gato sai, os ratos fazem a festa*
**TR** *Kedinin olmadığı yerde fareler cirit atar*
**RU** *Без кота мышам раздолье*

**"Once bitten, twice shy."**
**SI** *Osel gre samo enkrat na led*
**EE** *Teist korda sama reha otsa ei astu*
**RU** *Пуганая ворона куста боится*
**DE** *Ein gebranntes Kind scheut das Feuer*
**FR** *chat échaudé craint l'eau froide*
**SK** *Koho raz had uštipne, aj hlísty sa bojí*
**GR** *Όποιος καεί με τον χυλό, φυσάει και το γιαούρτι*

**"Pot calling the kettle black."**
**VN** *Chó chê mèo lắm lông*
**VE** *Cachicamo diciéndole a morrocoy conchudo*
**FR** *C'est le Roquefort qui dit au Camembert tue pue*
**JP** 猿の尻笑い

**"A mountain out of a molehill."**
**GR** *Πνίγομαι σε μια κουταλιά νερό*
**KR** 견문발검
**EG** صنع من الحبة قبة
**PL** *Robić z igły widły*
**ES** *Hacer una montaña de un grano de arena*
**IT** *Fare di una mosca un elefante*
**NL** *Van een mug een olifant maken*
**CZ** *Dělat z komára velblouda*
**BR** *Fazer tempestade em copo d'água*
**FR** *En faire tout un fromage*
**SE** *Göra en höna av en fjäder*

**Big Talk**
**IT** *Tutto fumo e niente arrosto*
**PL** *Krowa, która dużo ryczy, mało mleka daje*
**IN** *Jo garajte hai woh baraste nahi*
**ES** *Perro ladrador, poco mordedor*
**KR** 빈 수레가 요란하다

**"Birds of a feather . . . "**
**ES** *Cada oveja, con su pareja*
**PL** *Ciągnie swój do swego*
**RU** *Рыбак рыбака видит издалека*
**RU** *Гусь свинье не товарищ.*
**CZ** *Vrána k vráně sedá*
**FR** *Qui se ressemble s'assemble*
**PK** ڈ بېرن دمه په برۍ یېرۍ
**IN** चोर – चोर मौसेरे भा

**"Like father, like son."**
**AD** *De tal riu, tal aigua*
**ES** *De tal palo, tal astilla*
**JP** 蛙の子は蛙
**PT** *Filho de peixe, peixinho é*
**CN** 虎父無犬子
**FR** *Les chiens ne font pas des chats*

**"Beauty is in the eye . . . "**
**KR** 제 눈에 안경이다
**IQ** علف بايد به دهن بزى شيرين بياد
**ESP** *Hipopotaminon por hipopotamo*
**CN** 萝卜白菜, 各有所爱
**CN** 各花入各眼

**"Measure . . . , cut once."**
**FR** *Mesurer deux fois, couper une fois*
**NL** *Meet driemaal eer gij eens snijd*
**RO** *De şapte ori măsoară, o dată taie*
**EE** *üheksa korda mõõda, üks kord lõika*
**MT** *Qis mitt darba u aqta' darba*

**"Too many cooks . . ."**
**DE** *Viele Köche verderben den Brei*
**FI** *Mitä useampi kokki, sitä huonompi soppa*
**NL** *Veel koks bederven de brij*
**IT** *Troppi galli a cantare non fa mai giorno*
**VE** *Muchas manos en la olla ponen el caldo morado*
**VN** *Lắm thầy nhiều ma*
**KR** 사공이 많으면 배가 산으로 간다
**MK** *Mnogu babi, kilavo dete*
**AR** *Muchas manos en un plato hacen mucho garabato*
**CN** 三个和尚没水喝
**BR** *Cachorro que tem muito dono morre de fome*
**EG** القارب التي لها قائدان تغرق

**"Don't count your chickens . . ."**
**FI** *Älä nuolaise ennen kuin tipahtaa*
**KR** 김칫국부터 마시지 마라
**IT** *Non dire gatto se non ce l'hai nel sacco*
**AL** *Peshku në det,tigani në zjarr*
**DE** *Man soll den Tag nicht vor dem Abend loben*

**"A bird in the hand . . ."**
**SC** *'S fhearr iasg beag na bhith gun iasg idir*
**MY** *Yang dikejar tak dapat, yang dikendong berciciran*
**ZA** *Een is beter as niks*
**IT** *Meglio un uovo oggi che una gallina domain*

**"Out of the frying pan . . ."**
**TH** หนีเสือปะจระเข้
**DE** *Vom Regen in die Traufe*
**RU** *Волка бежа́л, да на медве́дя попа́л*
**IE** *Amach as na muineacha is isteach sna driseacha*
**RO** *Să fugi de dracu' și să dai de ta-su*
**VN** *Tránh vỏ dưa gặp vỏ dừa*

**"Two heads are better than one."**
**KR** 백지장도 맞들면 낫다
**VT** *Một cây làm chẳng nên non. Ba cây chụm lại nên hòn núi cao*
**JP** 三人寄れば文珠の知恵
**TU** *Bir elin nesi var iki elin sesi var*
**ES** *Cuatro ojos ven más que dos*
**IQ** با یک‌دست دو هندوانه نمی‌شود برداشت

**"You snooze, you lose."**
**PH** *Daig ng maagap ang taong masipag*
**IT** *Chi dorme non piglia pesci*
**CN** 先上山者隨意坐
**FR** *Le monde appartient à ceux qui se lèvent tôt*

**"When in Rome . . ."**
**VT** *Nhập gia tùy tục, nhập giang tùy khúc*
**BR** *Dance conforme a música*
**IN** जैसा देश वैसा भेष
**PL** *Jeśli wlazłeś między wrony, musisz krakać jak i one*
**TH** เข้าเมืองตาหลิ่วต้องหลิ่วตาตาม

**"Rome wasn't built in a day."**
**RU** *Москва не сразу строилась*
**FR** *Paris ne s'est pas fait en un jour*
**ESP** *Ne en unu tago elkreskis Kartago*

**"It's raining cats and dogs."**
**GR** *Βρέχει καρεκλοπόδαρα*
**AD** *Està plovent a bots i barrals*
**BR** *Chovem cobras e lagartos*
**CO** *Está lloviendo hasta maridos*
**FR** *Il pleut des cordes*
**CZ** *Padají trakaře*
**IS** *Það rignir eld og brennustein*
**WL** *Bwrw cyllyll a ffyrc*
**NO** *Det regner trollkjerringer*
**SK** *Padajú traktory*
**DK** *Det regner skomagerdrenge*
**PL** *Leje zabami*
**DE** *Es regnet junge Hunde*

**"The grass is always greener . . ."**
**IN** दूर के ढोल सुहावने लगते हैं
**CN** 這山望著那山高
**DE** *Die Kirschen aus Nachbars Garten schmecken immer besser*
**RU** *Соседняя очередь всегда движется быстрее*
**TR** *Komşunun tavuğu komşuya kaz görünür*
**CN** 他鄉月更圓
**SC** *'S e miann na lacha an loch air nach bi i*
**KR** 남의 떡이 더 커 보인다

**"A rock and a hard place."**
**EG** المأشة فكّي بين
**IT** Tra l'incudine e il martello
**SE** Mellan pest och kolera
**FR** Entre l'arbre et l'écorce
**FO** Sum lús millum tvær negl
**ES** Entre la espada y la pared
**JP** 板ばさみ
**IS** Milli tveggja elda
**AM** Երկու քարի արանքում

**"A few bad apples . . . "**
**CN** 一粒老鼠屎，壞了一鍋粥
**VT** Con sâu làm rầu nồi canh
**IN** एक सड़ी मछली सारे तालाब को गंदा कर देती है
**CZ** Jedna ovce prašivá celé stádo nakazí
**KE** Nazi mbovu harabu ya nzima

**"Selling like hotcakes."**
**NL** Ze verkopen als zoete broodjes
**TR** Peynir ekmek gibi gidiyor
**HU** Viszik mint a cukrot
**PT** Vender que nem água
**SE** Det säljer som smör
**ES** Se vende como pan caliente
**VT** Bán chạy như tôm tươi

**"Crying over spilt milk."**
**FI** Ei auta itku markkinoilla
**IN** अब पछताए होत क्या जब चड़िया चुग गई खेत.
**CN** 木已成舟
**FR** Les carottes sont cuites

**"It's all Greek to me."**
**IT** Questo per me è arabo
**EG** هندي تتكلم أنا هل
**IN** की मैं फ़ारसी बोल रहीं
**IQ** Urchíz burím Greek us
**GR** Εν τούρτζικα που μιλάς
**TR** Konuya Fransız kaldım
**FR** C'est de l'hébreu
**IL** בשבילי סינית זה
**CN** 呢啲係咪鬼畫符呀

# ACKNOWLEDGMENTS

Thank you to everyone who made this book possible—the people who contributed phrases and ideas, those who shared posts online, and most importantly the supporters on Kickstarter who brought an early version of this book into the real world. This book would not exist without these amazing people.

And of course, thanks to Catherine, Lyn, David, and Joe for their endless encouragement and being incredibly great.

# ABOUT THE AUTHOR

James Chapman is an illustrator and the author of *Sounds All Around*. He makes comics about language and has a PhD in physics for some reason. He lives in Manchester, UK.

**Follow James**

 @chapmangamo

 @chapmangamo

🌐 www.soundimals.com

**A WORLD OF WISDOM**

Andrews McMeel Publishing
a division of Andrews McMeel Universal
1130 Walnut Street, Kansas City, Missouri 64106

www.andrewsmcmeel.com

21 22 23 24 25 TEN 10 9 8 7 6 5 4 3 2 1

ISBN: 978-1-5248-6146-9

Library of Congress Control Number: 2021934469

Made by:
1010 Printing International, Ltd.
Address and place of production:
1010 Avenue, Xia Nan Industrial District,
Yuan Zhou Town, Bo Luo County
Guang Don Province, China 615123
1st printing – 6/21/21

Editor: Allison Adler
Art Director: Tiffany Meairs
Production Editor: Jasmine Lim
Production Manager: Tamara Haus